Small Miracles

Small Miracles

The Extraordinary Stories of Ordinary People
Touched by God

Tom Sheridan

ZondervanPublishingHouse
Grand Rapids, Michigan

A Division of HarperCollinsPublishers

Small Miracles
Copyright © 1996 by Tom Sheridan

Requests for information should be addressed to:

ZondervanPublishingHouse
Grand Rapids, Michigan 49530

Library of Congress Cataloging-in-Publication Data

Sheridan, Tom, 1943–
    Small miracles : the extraordinary stories of ordinary people touched by God /
Tom Sheridan.
       p.   cm.
    ISBN: 0-310-20793-2
    1. Miracles—Case studies. 2. Christian biography. I. Title.
BT97.2.S54 1996
231.7'3—dc 00   96-16499
                                               CIP

This edition printed on acid-free paper and meets the American National Standards
Institute Z39.48 standard.

Interior design by Sherri Hoffman

Printed in the United States of America

---

97 98 99 00 01 02 03 /❖ QF/ 10 9 8 7 6 5 4 3

This book of miracles is dedicated to the person in my life who has been the link, the connection, between all the other miracles. She showed me faith when I had none. She taught me—and continues to teach me—relationship when I couldn't always understand or appreciate it.

She has parented our children, healed minds, bodies, and souls. She has changed the world. She certainly changed mine. This book, and indeed all I do, is dedicated to Kathy, who has shown me who God is and what a miracle is.

I will remember the deeds of the LORD;
 yes, I will remember your miracles of long ago.
I will meditate on all your works
 and consider all your mighty deeds.

Your ways, O God, are holy.
 What god is so great as our God?
You are the God who performs miracles;
 you display your power among the peoples.

Ps. 77:11–14

Contents

Acknowledgments

*This book is filled with miracles. These small miracles are stories that have been told to me by the very people who experienced them and who, in the process, were touched by the power of God. I am indebted to them for the opportunity to become, if only for a brief moment, a part of their lives. Their inspiration and their words will shine bolts of lightning into dark places of people's hearts for years to come; indeed, all who read these stories will understand what it means to be truly touched by miracles.

But something more must be said about the many, many miracle stories that aren't on these pages. It would not be right to ignore the hundreds of others who wrote. Their stories and miracles and insights and glimpses of faith are no less valuable, no less real. It simply is not possible to wrap up all the good works of God into a single (or even a multiple) book. Nor am I the first author to recognize that reality. The gospel writer John said much the same thing: "Jesus did many other things as well. If every one of them were written down, I suppose that even the whole world would not have room for the books that would be written" (John 21:25).

So to those whose words are part of this book and to all those whose words could not be, thank you.

Deepest gratitude must go to my family, especially my wife and partner, Kathy, whose unbending support and encouragement allowed the miracle project to continue. Thanks also to Tom Artz, who, as friend and agent, did much to bring this idea and others to completion, and to Chuck Crowder, friend, physicist, and skilled proofreader, for his faith-filled, enthusiastic, and accurate assistance.

Real People, Real Stories

Dear Friend,

The stories you are about to read are the stories of ordinary people who have experienced extraordinary events in their lives. Because of their faith—and even sometimes despite their apparent lack of faith—they have attributed these extraordinary events to a touch of the divine. In other words, a miracle.

Skeptics may be disappointed that the miracles here aren't quantified or dissected or even independently proven. Investigative reporters will look here for confirmation they are unlikely to find. Some of the events recounted here might, by another measure, be dismissed as ordinary events, mere coincidences that impacted people extraordinarily.

And perhaps there is no difference. A miracle may be not so much what happens to us but how—and if—we see in it the hand of God.

On the pages of this book are scores of stories. They tell of miracles of war, miracles of flowers, of angels and faith, of healing, and of recognizing the presence of God. There are tales of being lost and then found, and stories of disasters in which God was present. However, at the root of it all, at the bottom of every miracle, is the sense of relationship with God or with others, and the sense that people have been changed.

These are stories of families in need, of couples in celebration, of parents and children, of memories and hope. These are stories of the sometimes desperate, sometimes joyous human condition and of how people found their way through their experiences. Some are stories that flow out of a relationship with God. Others are the result of that relationship. Still others are the beginning of such a relationship. In each case, people were changed somehow, because that change is an essential element in a miracle. It is, in a sense, why miracles happen.

It is also why such events—such miracles—are recalled so vividly years and decades after the fact.

These are the stories of people who have experienced a special touch of God. Yet, to a person, they will tell you that they are not special, that the touch is not unique, not for them alone. It is for anyone—for us all—when we can see beyond a life situation.

The most extraordinary thing about miracles is that they happen most often to ordinary people. That's the common link. These people aren't all kings or celebrities. They aren't all learned and wise. Nor are they even all religious or especially pious. They are quite ordinary.

So why should stories of ordinary people—ordinary people like us—be so intriguing? Perhaps it's because of their very ordinariness. We all seek the encouragement to believe that life is something more than a day-to-day existence, that faith is real and God is truly a part of the world. The miracle stories that ordinary people share are proof that it can happen. And if it can happen to them, it can happen to us.

The prospect of gathering small miracles appeared daunting at first, but in the end it was wondrously easy. I wrote letters to the editors of weekly newspapers all around the United States, from Maine to Hawaii, from Alaska to the Virgin Islands. I also sent letters to Canadian newspapers. I'm thankful to the editors and to the many congregations of all denominations across northern Illinois that placed the "Small Miracles" note in their church bulletins. (The request was a simple one. See page 187.)

The search for, and the recounting of, miracles is not something that belongs to one religion or denomination. It remains a reality that is common to many faiths. The stories in this book came from all over. They came from small farm towns, suburbs, and big cities. They came from mountains and seashores, from more than forty states and at least two countries. Nearly two thousand people responded, and miracles still grace my mailbox. I expect—indeed hope—this will continue.

One of the most surprising things, at first, was the unabashed willingness of people to share themselves and their stories with me, a stranger. Some of these tales are obviously well-worn, having been told and retold many times by the person who lived them. Others are fresh and alive and as new as a shiny penny. Some people told me things they'd never before told anyone.

Many who wrote said they were glad to have been asked to share their stories. For instance: "It's good to hear about someone else who believes in small miracles," wrote Barb Darling from Arvada, Colorado. "When I was a child and a young adult, I tended to think of God as being busy with great mysteries and miracles, like healing very faithful 'religious types.' But now I have had the privilege of knowing a much more personal God, a friend who cares about my mundane, everyday life. I don't believe that he necessarily intervenes in every small happenstance but that he somehow has ... my dreams and my desires, my terrors and my anxieties, in his heart and his hand."

In letter after letter, from all parts of the country, there was often a common phrase. It went something like this: "I saw your letter and felt compelled to write ..." The word "compelled" was used over and over, in letters from just about everywhere.

I think there was a reason for that, a very simple reason. It's because miracles aren't really miracles until they've been told.

That's a pretty strong statement. It is, however, the sense behind much of human understanding: every time we tell a story, we own it a little more. And the stories of life that have become miracles to us need to be told and owned.

That's hardly a divine revelation or even a particularly brilliant one. It was even said long ago by Johann Wolfgang von Goethe, the celebrated author of the masterpiece play *Faust*, in which the hero experiences a miracle of his own. In the play, Faust, the ultimate pleasure-seeker, is saved by the grace of God, not because he deserves it but because it's the nature of God to save sinners. That is a very real truth behind the miracles of everyday life: we neither deserve them nor are owed them. They are a gift from God. They are a gift that we celebrate by telling and retelling the story.

Goethe said it this way: "All truly wise thoughts have been thought already thousands of times; but to make them truly our own, we must think them over again honestly, until they take root in our personal experience."

⟋⟍

In Acts, Peter explains the irresistible call to proclaim the Good News:

> Then they called them in again and commanded them not to speak or teach at all in the name of Jesus. But Peter and John replied, "Judge for yourselves whether it is right in God's sight to obey you rather than God. For we cannot help speaking about what we have seen and heard." (ACTS 4:18–20)

The ability to take God's touches in our lives and make them truly our own—to recognize them for what they are and to share them—is what this book is all about.

Miracle stories are the ultimate in people watching. At a bench on Main Street or in the mall, miracle stories are the same—we get to watch God go by. The power of such stories is to instruct, encourage, and lead, something a dry treatise on faith often fails to do. This is faith alive—blood-pumping, arm-waving alive.

When I first had the idea to ask people—everyday, ordinary people—about miracles they had seen or experienced, I had no idea what to expect.

I belong to a cynical profession. I'm a newspaperman. I've been a writer and reporter, an editor, and a daily columnist. In each of these capacities, I've listened often to the ravings of people who told me unimaginable stories about incomprehensible things. Only rarely, however, were those stories about faith. More likely, they were about their own supposed human greatness and assumed human accomplishments.

The news business seems to have one guiding principle: Believe nothing you hear and only half of what you see. A familiar cliché is, "If your mother says she loves you, check it out." Since it's more difficult to check out whether God loves you, perhaps that's why many of my breed find faith a challenge. I did, for a long time. All in all, it's not a very fertile ground for miracles. But after reading hundreds of adventures from all over the United States and Canada, I'm reconfirmed in my belief that miracles need to be claimed. That was something Jesus recognized:

> Now on his way to Jerusalem, Jesus traveled along the border between Samaria and Galilee. As he was going into a village, ten

men who had leprosy met him. They stood at a distance and called out in a loud voice, "Jesus, Master, have pity on us!"

When he saw them, he said, "Go, show yourselves to the priests." And as they went, they were cleansed.

One of them, when he saw he was healed, came back, praising God in a loud voice. He threw himself at Jesus' feet and thanked him—and he was a Samaritan.

Jesus asked, "Were not all ten cleansed? Where are the other nine? Was no one found to return and give praise to God except this foreigner?" Then he said to him, "Rise and go; your faith has made you well." (LUKE 17:11–19)

The bits and pieces of their lives that people shared have convinced me that we needn't be worried when God seems distant. Not only is he close, there are hundreds and thousands and perhaps millions just waiting to be asked to tell how close he is. These miracles are the stories of faith that we tell each other. They are how we recognize and appreciate the presence of God in our midst.

As one woman wrote: "The more I think of my life, the more miracles I see." Then she proceeded to tell me several.

It's been a powerful, awesome experience to be on the receiving end of such stories. I have seen that such miracles all have one thing in common, no matter what the subject. That is that miracles change people. None of the people who told me their stories are the same as they were before. And they'll be the first to admit it. Something happened. Something powerful. Something extraordinary.

So read and enjoy.

—*Tom Sheridan*
Spring 1996

One

❧

Miracle of the Monarchs

The last thing JoAnn expected was a miracle. The last thing she wanted was a miracle. Pain, anguish, and desperation do that to people. JoAnn was angry and bitter because her daughter, a very beautiful part of her life, had been snatched away. And no one, not even God, seemed to understand how much it hurt.

"When I saw the request for small miracles," JoAnn said, "I had to share mine with you."

It happened a few years ago, she said. "I lost my beautiful, twenty-four-year-old daughter, Suzanne." The young woman had suffered a massive convulsion and cardiac arrest and had slipped into a coma. JoAnn said she prayed and prayed then for a miracle, "but it was not to be." Suzanne died twelve days later.

"I went crazy with grief and sorrow," said JoAnn. "Two weeks after her death, I remained lost in pain and misery. I didn't want to be part of this world any longer. Why, I asked myself, hadn't God taken me instead?"

JoAnn explained that although she had been raised within a faithful family, she had been away from her church for years. In her desperation, she returned to prayer and the familiar strains of the Sunday service in her Illinois hometown church, seeking peace and acceptance of this terrible tragedy. "One Sunday soon after Suzanne died, I returned home from church and found my husband swimming merrily in our pool. Immediately I resented him for being able to still enjoy himself while I continued suffering. From the pool, he politely called for me to join him."

She was brimming with anger and hurt and woundedness. All sorts of vile and nasty thoughts roared through her mind. Just as she was ready to spit out some words she surely would have regretted later, something strange happened. Seemingly out of nowhere, a beautiful monarch butterfly appeared, fluttered up to JoAnn, and settled on her leg.

Amazed, JoAnn thought later, *I was wearing white shorts and a white shirt. I don't look like a flower, nor do I smell like one.* Yet the magnificent black-and-gold insect didn't seem to mind; it simply continued to perch there.

"The monarch stayed and I walked with it still on my leg, its wings quivering ever so slightly, to the edge of the pool. I yelled for my husband to look. We both stared in wonder for what must have been several minutes, not quite believing what we were seeing." The butterfly then launched itself and flew away—up, up, up, and was lost to their sight.

Butterflies are beautiful, a wonder to behold. But butterflies by themselves aren't miraculous. Except perhaps in the broadest sense of creation. So what's the miracle?

JoAnn explained that Suzanne had once had a hobby creating monarch butterflies out of yarn. It was how she learned to crochet. "She made dozens and dozens of them and gave them to family and friends as gifts," JoAnn said. In many ways, the monarch became Suzanne's symbol for the beauty she helped share with others.

JoAnn said, "I like to think that she somehow wanted me to know she was safe with the Lord and for me to get on with my life." Later a clergy friend explained that the butterfly is a sign of resurrection and new life. "I feel very fortunate to have been touched by the hand of God," JoAnn said.

For JoAnn and her family, Suzanne's death dashed their hopes for a miracle. After all, didn't God refuse to save her? Yet it wasn't a yellow butterfly that landed and clung to JoAnn's leg. It wasn't a moth or a bird or a boll weevil. It was a monarch, the only thing that would have had the powerful, awesome meaning it did. Such meaning is wherever we can find it. Jesus understood our sometimes reluctant belief:

> Do not believe me unless I do what my Father does. But if I do it, even though you do not believe me, believe the miracles, that you may know and understand that the Father is in me, and I in the Father. (JOHN 10:37–38)

But was it a miracle, really? Or just a coincidence?

You and I aren't qualified to judge. All we can do is recognize that for JoAnn and her family, the arrival of the monarch was a miracle, an awesome one that affirmed faith in the midst of crisis.

It's too easy to dismiss such an occurrence as a coincidence. It's too easy to look back at an insight, a hunch, a happenstance, and say, "It just happened." And maybe it did. What cannot be denied is that JoAnn believed. And no one can take that away from her.

❧

Lord of Life

Lord, you fill the world around us with your creations.
We are surrounded by signs and wonders of your presence,
   signs and wonders which sometimes escape our notice.
Help us always to recognize and appreciate
   your presence in the world in which we spend our days.
You are a God of signs. You are a God of wonders.
Help us to be open to seeing those wonders of a God of Life.
Amen.

Two

᧞

You Dare Call *That* a Miracle?

The voice from across the church vestibule after the service was clear, insistent, and agitated.

"It sounded," said the voice, which was attached to a young and earnest man, "like you were saying that the miracle of the multiplication of loaves and fish didn't really happen!"

The comment was directed to the preacher of the morning, who had just completed a sermon on the marvelous story of Jesus and his disciples feeding the multitude by bringing forth a few loaves of bread and a couple of fish. The comment and the man who asked it are memorable because I was that preacher. I've thought often about that episode since. It gave me a tremendous insight into how we understand the role of God, and miracles, in our lives.

The core of the sermon that offended him so went like this:

᧞

"This gospel story—this familiar miracle of the feeding of the five thousand—is the only miracle story of Jesus to appear in all four gospels. We have to imagine the scene to understand why. There is a vast multitude of people spread out on the hillside—five thousand men and at least that many women and children. They've been listening to Jesus tell them about the kingdom of God, about the healing touch of a God who cares, about the presence of God in their midst. And this had gone on all day. The people are hungry, hot, and thirsty.

"That event must have had a tremendous impact for all of the evangelists to include it in their accounts. Undoubtedly, it's because the gospel is a story of connectedness. Jesus was not a dispassionate, isolated preacher. He didn't talk down to people. He shared stories of life with them, stories they could relate to. He was connected to his listeners by the life they shared.

"The gospel is a story of compassion. Jesus certainly saw that the crowds who had followed him for so many hours were tired and hungry. And ultimately he fed them. But first he blessed them. Jesus knew that in the crowd before him there were doubters, skeptics, unbelievers, and just plain people along for the ride—not unlike today. But still, he fed their souls with a blessing before he fed their bodies with bread and fish.

"The gospel is a story of responsibility. It's a sense not only of responsibility taken but of responsibility given. It was clear that Jesus had a sense of responsibility for those people who had followed him onto the mountainside. Yet it was a responsibility he was willing to share with his disciples and ultimately with the people themselves.

"The gospel is a story of challenge. When Jesus talked to the crowds about the kingdom of God, he recognized that they had the power of decision. The kingdom would happen, he said, but for people to be part of it would require some action, some acknowledgment, some choice, on their part. In other words, Jesus didn't offer easy answers. He challenged those who would follow him to make choices, to wrestle with their faith, to do what they thought they never could.

"The gospel is a story of reveling in growth. Jesus honored growth, and celebrated response to his challenges. He reveled in his followers getting a glimmer of what the future might hold. He was enthused when they sensed the power of faith, or an understanding of the true mission of the kingdom of God.

"And there's more, too. There is the sense of belonging to one another, a sense of family.

"What happened on that hillside that so few fish and so few loaves became enough to fill the needs of so many? The clue, if you're into detective stories, is this: where did the twelve baskets come from to hold all the leftovers?

> When they had all had enough to eat, he said to his disciples, "Gather the pieces that are left over. Let nothing be wasted." So they gathered them and filled twelve baskets with the pieces of the five barley loaves left over by those who had eaten. (JOHN 6:12–13)

"People can be selfish and distrustful. And the tradition in those days was for travelers away from home, even for relatively short distances, to bring food and drink along. There were no 7-Elevens in that neighborhood. It was usually just enough for themselves, because to display that food was to invite others to share it, and that meant maybe not having enough to go around.

"So there in the crowd on the hillside, it remained put away, hidden. But when Jesus blessed and began to share what little he and his disciples had, it encouraged others to do the same. That was when the crowd brought out their own traveling fare—flat, unleavened loaves and dried lake fish—and the baskets it was carried in. When it was over . . . well, you know the rest. They had lots of leftovers—and lots of baskets to carry the leftovers in.

"The miracle here is not five loaves of bread and a few small fish. The miracle is that we can be convinced by the power of God to open ourselves and share not only what we have but who we are, to share from our core, to share even those things that we have hidden away. That's what happened on the hillside; Jesus knew when to trust that people would see that God was working and respond.

"We are the descendants of the people on that hillside, the spiritual descendants. We are the five thousand men and the uncounted women and children who are—still today—hot and hungry and thirsty. And Jesus is still among us. But the miracle isn't the physical creation of loaves and fish and baskets. The miracle then, as now, is that sense of connectedness, that sense of responsibility, that sense of compassion, that sense of challenge, and finally, that reveling in growth."

❧

It was into that charged atmosphere that the earnest, agitated, and insistent voice repeated itself: "It sounded like you were saying that the miracle of the multiplication of loaves and fish didn't really happen!"

Meaning, of course: "What's all this stuff about people carrying their own food? Didn't Jesus wave a divine, magical wand over his disciples' bits and pieces of food and bring into existence a bakery full of bread and a hatchery full of fish?"

Well, multiplication surely did take place. But not exactly like that. The miracle was not so much the changing of things but the changing of hearts and minds and attitudes. However, understanding that reality can be an uncomfortable stretch for someone steeped in the tradition that God is a magician, walking among his people and doing parlor tricks.

Witness the voice's response that morning: "But to me," it said, "that was the main idea." Meaning that if Jesus didn't do that "magical act," why are we in church? Why should we have faith? Why is this special? Why should we remember?

Which is too bad. Does the sense that Jesus changed hearts rather than loaves shake faith or threaten our understanding of miracles? It shouldn't. And for most people it doesn't. Most of us believe that God continues to work miracles today, just like the one on that mountainside. We may not always understand how—or even recognize when—but we believe.

George H. Gallup Jr. understands that reality. Gallup, the nation's premier pollster, has been tracking such things for decades, along with the more traditional subjects of polls—politics, lifestyles, and attitudes. Americans' belief in miracles has been consistent, Gallup explained from his office in Princeton, New Jersey. His polls bear this out. Asked in 1988 if they believed miracles are still performed today by the power of God, 51 percent of those polled said they agreed completely. Only 6 percent said they didn't believe. When asked again in 1994, 79 percent reported they believed in miracles. During an interview for this book, Gallup counted himself among their number.

Gallup, long active in small Christian groups—covenant groups, he calls them—described a miracle as not necessarily a physical manifestation of God but more likely something concerning relationship, either with God or others. "For many people," he said, "it's seen in dramatic turnarounds, in healed relationships, and in a growing awareness of God in their lives."

The impact of religion—and faith—on the nation has long been a passion of Gallup. As codirector of the Gallup Organization, he followed his father into the family's business of keeping track of the pulse of America. But because he has had a deep and abiding interest in faith—he once planned for a life in the Episcopal ministry—Gallup has added that flavor to his own polling.

In the mid–1970s, while America was undergoing a sense of crisis about its spiritual identity, Gallup cofounded the Princeton Religion Research Center (P.O. Box 389, Princeton, NJ 08542). The PRRC uses Gallup's polling techniques to grasp a sense of the faith of America. The organization's monthly bulletin, *Emerging Trends,* is a key barometer of what Americans believe about prayer and about God. It examines churchgoing habits and how people sense that God has become active in their lives. Gallup calls that latter event a "religious awakening." He has written extensively about faith issues, mostly based on his experience in polling Americans about their beliefs.

Indeed, Gallup said, the PRRC polls reflect an even greater belief in miracles than in angels. Such belief is widespread. More people have been touched by miracles—when they think about it—than have known (or believed they have known) angels. Witness a separate poll taken in mid–1994 by the respected *Orange County Register,* one of California's major daily newspapers. The poll reported that from almost six hundred responses, 87 percent believed in miracles.

In Gallup's polling, the highest numbers of miracle believers—84 percent—came from "baby boomers," those aged thirty to forty-nine, but other age groups were represented only marginally less. Gender, race, region, education, and even household income do not greatly affect the conviction that miracles are a valid and important part of our world. Nor is there any statistical difference in belief between Protestant denominations and Roman Catholics. It's true that slightly more women than men believe, and Gallup reports that those for whom religion is important are twice as likely to recognize miracles.

While most Americans profess a belief in miracles—defined as believing in the power of God to change lives—many of us, like the man after the sermon, prefer to keep such changes outside ourselves, not to internalize them.

In that sense, many of us share a view of miracles that is more centered in the physical world. While these are most common in the Old Testament, there are also New Testament examples.

Once upon a time, miracles were glorious, expansive, tremendous events so huge and remarkable that they are still read about today—the burning bush, the voice from the sky, the parting of the Red Sea, Jesus calming the storm. We're heard about them all.

In those days, God appeared to change things, not people. Oh, the people were changed, all right. Even Scripture bears that out—hearts of stone were removed and hearts of flesh restored—but it wasn't always recognized that way. Call it a development issue. Because humankind is forever growing in understanding, so too is our response to the awareness of God in our lives.

The stories we tell our children about God are usually long on love and images and appropriately short on theology. God is someone "out there," perhaps watching, making sure we do the right thing. And perhaps he is prepared to punish us for doing the wrong things. But adults are supposed to grow into the understanding that God is here, and now so is the kingdom.

It's not much different from other things children learn about life.

Once when my son Mark was small, he was convinced that I worked on the commuter train—riding all day back and forth between our suburb and downtown Chicago. What else should he expect; that was the sum of his experience. He frequently would be in the car when I was dropped off at the station. And he would sometimes be there to help pick me up again. Besides, he knew about trains; he'd seen them, even ridden them.

But he had never been at my office. That was beyond his childish comprehension. I could tell him, of course. But he was unable to understand the concept.

That's not unlike how we teach our children about God.

We don't really teach them about theology. We teach them at their level. The message of love is good, no matter if we use an image they can relate to—perhaps an elderly gent with long hair and flowing beard who's always watching us. And of course, we begin to teach them the rules about religion. None of this is bad, you understand, but neither is it at an adult level.

And naturally, there are the stories, those wonderful Bible stories, like Noah's epic adventure on an ark filled with two of every kind of squawking, squealing, flying, walking, and slithering thing. That's a wonderful tale, a nice and fun children's story, probably the all-time favorite. But rarely do we share with children the sense of God's promise and salvation that is the core of Noah's tale of faithfulness, obedience, hope, and rescue. Yet that's what the writer wanted us to know; that's what he wanted the ancients to understand when he set the words down. That was certainly the message God wanted to get across by inspiring the story. It wasn't about some jaunty little cruise with a fun menagerie. It was a great deal more than that.

That understanding will come later—hopefully—when a child can appreciate it developmentally. Sometimes, though, our development ceases and we get stuck. Then, even for adults, Noah's story remains something childish and never becomes a metaphor of the powerful love God has for his faithful people.

Even the poignant parables of Jesus, told to his followers to illuminate the message of salvation and to encourage appropriate behavior, lose the flavor of faith if we don't see them as more than simple stories. We sometimes reduce them to children's tales and miss the adult message Jesus was offering.

Churches that fail to help their congregations make the transition from child's story to adult understanding have missed out. A very insightful clergy friend once summed it up better than I could. He said, "Jesus played with children and taught adults; too often our churches teach children and play with adults."

When that happens, miracles are overlooked and people fail to recognize that God is present and active in their daily lives. God gets relegated to dry and dusty words on a Bible page or special effects on a movie screen.

Perhaps no one understood that better than Saint Paul, who recognized that the way he had comprehended God in the Hebrew Scriptures was not the only understanding possible. He recognized that it was time for the child to grow up: "When I was a child, I talked like a child, I thought like a child, I reasoned like a child. When I became a man, I put childish ways behind me" (I Cor. 13:11).

How important is our ability to experience miracles—or to be aware that we have been changed by such events?

George Gallup Jr.: "People who have an empirical reason to believe hold their faith more strongly than those whose belief comes from rational or authoritarian reasons." Such people, he said, who have experienced a touch of the divine in their lives, are more likely to be in the "vanguard of their churches."

As part of the increasing "new surge of belief" that Gallup's polls have evidenced, miracles and prayer are a key to keeping faith alive and current. To believe that miracles happened "once upon a time" but not today is to practice a faith more appropriate to a museum than a church. Either our God is active in our lives or he's not.

This is reflected in the things for which people seek heavenly assistance. Americans most frequently ask for God's help—a miracle, perhaps—in seeking strength or guidance when facing a challenge (92 percent), in seeking help when dealing with a personal problem (80 percent), and in seeking comfort when frightened (79 percent). Most of the miracles detailed in this book will fit into one or more of those categories.

Why should we seek to believe in miracles of relationship and prayer and rescue? Of God's touches that change people, not just events or things?

For many people, these miraculous touches of a loving God soften the hard edges between the sacred and the secular, creating a bridge of sorts that allows those too-often separate areas to flow together. Certainly God never meant for us to keep those two sides of our nature apart. It's the mission of faith to draw them together—to permit God to be an everyday part of life, not to exist for only an hour on Sunday morning.

For the ancients, the visible was more impressive than the subtle. That's not unlike children or, for that matter, many of us today. Which is why magic is so attractive to children.

As recreated on the big screen by the legendary filmmaker Cecil B. deMille *(The Ten Commandments)*, the parting of the Red Sea is impressive to behold, recounting the biblical words:

> Then Moses stretched out his hand over the sea, and all that night the LORD drove the sea back with a strong east wind and turned it into dry land. The waters were divided, and the Israelites went through the sea on dry ground, with a wall of water on their right and on their left. (Ex. 14:21–22)

Special effects make such miracles a powerful spectacle on the screen. But it's unfortunate that this can give us a mistaken understanding of miracles. We grow up to believe that miracles are always rare and awesome things, that they can only happen when the music swells, the skies darken, and the camera pans across a vast assemblage of amazed and awestruck humans. Then the music quickens and the special effects take over.

But is that a miracle? Or rather, is that how a miracle was?

With apologies to Indiana Jones, Charlton Heston, and even George Burns, the answer is: not necessarily.

Playwright George Bernard Shaw was no great fan of faith, but he was a keen observer of human nature. And he made this valuable comment: "In heaven, an angel is nobody in particular." He might have said the same thing about miracles. The lesson is that we look for angels—and by extension, miracles—to be superspecial, unique, and unusual, when in fact they're around us all the time.

Ultimately, it's not the fact that miracles can change things—even the depth of the Red Sea—that ought to impress us. It's that miracles ultimately change people. That's the bottom line: miracles must have an impact on human hearts. Otherwise, they remain a fancy parlor trick. The purpose of the dash across the Red Sea was not to make a show of force or to give C. B. deMille material for a movie thirty-five hundred years later. It was to make the connection between God and his people understood, to reveal that this is a God who saves, not just a God who does magic.

Besides not being magic, there are lots of other things a miracle isn't.

A miracle isn't the suspension of the natural order of things. But sometimes it may appear that way.

A miracle isn't necessarily a grand and glorious flash of divine power. But sometimes it could be.

A miracle isn't always a pivotal event that shifts the course of humankind. But it always shifts the course of an individual's life.

What is a miracle? Well, lots of things. And lots of people have lots of their own ideas about what a miracle is. This book is full of them.

For instance:

A miracle is a coincidence in which God chooses to be anonymous.

A miracle is also a coincidence in which God tips his hand.

A miracle is the ability to discover success in failure. Or to notice wonder amid disaster. Or even to recognize the uncommon in the common.

Even a small miracle is no small thing. And people need miracles as much as miracles need people.

The reality is this: what we perceive to be miraculous, probably is.

But doesn't the sense that miracles are all around us seem to trivialize them? Whatever happened to words like "awesome" and "majesty"?

There is a tendency these days to make God less than he is. That is, after all, an attempt at connectedness. But it is also a danger. Neither God nor his works ought to be trivialized. Some of the stories on the pages of this book might seem to some readers to do that.

But they don't.

Perhaps the special effects we've come to associate with miracles don't happen as often as we might wish. Bushes don't burst into flame, voices don't shout from the skies, and piles of bread don't appear in the midst of hungry crowds.

But people are changed. People are pulled out of themselves. People are rescued, saved. People are infused with faith, thunderstruck at the sense that God was there. People are compelled to share their stories of the touch of God, sometimes immediately and constantly, sometimes years later.

So how can we spot a miracle? How do we determine whether one just happened? How do we judge what is a miracle and what isn't?

Beware! There's a danger to judging the miracles of others—saying this one is good, this one isn't, this is too trivial, this one could have just been a coincidence, and so on.

During the few months when letters describing miracles were arriving at my mailbox from all over the nation, my wife, Kathy, was confined to a wheelchair. She had suffered a terrible accident that shattered the bones of her leg. It meant weeks in the hospital and months more before she could even begin to walk.

As she recovered, the daily mail quickly became a highlight. Since she often had little else to occupy her time and take her mind off the constant pain in her severely injured leg, she pored over the letters that flooded in each afternoon.

It was uplifting. It was powerful. But she tells the story of making judgments as she read each letter. "That was a great miracle," she would say, putting down one particularly powerful letter and picking up another. "Well," she would think next, "that one wasn't such a big deal."

Finally the irony struck her. "I could just hear God saying to me, 'Who do you think you are, Kathy Sheridan, to judge my miracles?'" She said she realized that it didn't matter if the story in this letter or that one seemed like a miracle to her. What mattered was that it was an event so meaningful that it impacted people's lives—so much so that even years later they were still talking about it.

"From then on," she explained, "every letter was full of the power of God."

And she helped develop some guidelines for how to look for a miracle in yourself and in others. To experience God's touch—or to recall a time he touched you in the past—stay open to inspiration. Trust. Sense the excitement of a moment. Recognize the glimmers of faith peeking out from beneath the clouds. Reflect at the end of each day: "Was God part of my life?" Pray. Hope. Love. And let yourself be loved. Don't be afraid of trouble; in order to heal, we must first hurt. And perhaps most of all, expect a miracle. Never lose sight of the fact that God still does perform miracles. Sometimes he changes things; sometimes he changes events. But most often he changes people.

It was healing for Kathy to hear the good news that God was touching so many people. It helped her through a difficult period. Was it a miracle that hundreds and hundreds of stories of healings, of awakenings, of touched relationships and wondrous happenings, were delivered at a time when she was most in need of seeing them and being reminded of the love of God?

You know, I believe it was.

Many, O LORD my God,
   are the wonders you have done.
The things you planned for us
   no one can recount to you;
were I to speak and tell of them,
   they would be too many to declare.
                 —Ps. 40:5

Three

❧

The Miracle of Healing

"*If*" is a great word. It packs a lot of meaning into a tiny bundle. "If" explores the whole range of possibilities. It's great for asking a question without really spelling it out.

Our children play the "if" game a lot. And they don't always use words. It's all in the behavior. It's all part of growing up and away. "If I do this or act this way, what's going to happen? If I run and play in the street, if I do what you tell me not to, if I challenge your authority, will you still care? If I somehow disappoint you, will you still love me? Can I believe that? Will you still make me safe?"

And it's not just our children who do that. We do it as well. We do it with each other in our relationships, and we do it with our God. When we let it, "if" can become a wonderful sign of trust and a powerful image of hope. And there is no one who has not, during life, found themselves in a place without trust, a place without love. So very often, the question we ask is: "If there's a God and if he cares, can he—will he—cure this affliction?" Sometimes that affliction is a disease; sometimes it's a human condition; sometimes it's a particularly difficult slice of life itself.

As humans, our ability to trust in others—and in God—is some-times directly related not to the other but to how we feel about ourselves, about how we are able to experience—and trust—love that is unconditional. You see, most of us don't have a good track record with being loved unconditionally. Someone somewhere in our past put strings on love. That is what makes us pull back from it, makes us doubt it, makes us wonder: "Am I lovable? If I do this or that, will you love me? Will you heal me of my afflictions—whether they are within me or without?" We are too often afraid to trust that God cares enough to answer our cry for help.

Let me tell you a story about trust and about hope and about "if." It's about a healing of a sort we might not expect—but a healing just the same. The teller of the story—the woman who experienced it—still remembers a hand-to-mouth, paycheck-to-paycheck experience during the early 1970s, when she and her family lived in a western state. Her name is Susan. She lives in Nebraska now.

Back then, Susan and her husband had seven lively, boisterous children at home. Cash was always scarce, and she admitted that sometimes she'd write checks and hope there would be money in their account to cover them when they hit the bank. Sometimes they made it and sometimes they didn't. When they didn't, her embarrassment was real and uncomfortable.

Susan told me she had good friends who were adopting a Vietnamese orphan and were going to pick him up at a nearby airport. This was another couple who had their hands full—they already had six children of various sizes, colors, and handicaps. The boy who was soon to be the newest member of their family suffered from various afflictions. He was blind and probably mentally handicapped. Susan said her friends didn't expect any cures for him; being in their family would be enough. They loved him and would care for him. Yet they too lived from paycheck to paycheck.

As her friends left to pick up their most recent precious gift from God, Susan said she asked the Lord to inspire her to do that which would be most helpful, most healing, to the family. She said it came to her immediately that having a nice supper ready for them when they all returned would be most comforting. But she had no cash.

Oh, she said, she could write a check, but it would overdraw their account, and she was understandably hesitant to do that. All the way to the grocery store, she struggled with the idea. It seemed right, but God surely wouldn't want her to write a bum check, would he? Even for the healing act of warming hearts and filling bellies?

Yet, she said, her stumbling feet led her down the aisles with a cart full of meat and vegetables. At the checkout, she gritted her teeth and wrote the check.

She felt good—and she felt bad. Good that she was trusting that what she was doing was blessed by God. And more than a little afraid that she couldn't completely believe in that trust.

On the way home with her "good deed groceries," she stopped off at the post office to pick up her family's mail. Among the envelopes was a refund check she'd forgotten all about. The amount was so close to the amount of the check she'd written at the store that the difference hardly mattered. She said, "That was scary!"

She told me, "I don't believe that God asks us to overdraw our bank accounts. But he does ask us to risk and to listen and—often—to be rescued." When the friends returned with their new son, the pot roast was done, it was welcomed, and it was devoured. Susan said, "I'll never forget that special time."

That's a very little story that may mean very little to you. But it's a story of "ifs." "If I do this, will you still love me? If I do this, can I trust that it's going to be okay?" That's a promise that is echoed throughout faith and throughout Scripture. It's a promise that allows us to walk through the valley of "ifs," the valley in which we try to remember that God loves us unconditionally and that he promises to heal the ills of our lives. That's easy to forget, because we aren't always ready to believe we deserve such love. In a very real sense, it's the acceptance of a healing touch.

For us as adults, it's not the questions that our children might ask—or even that we might have asked as children: "If I do this thing that's not right, can I trust that you'll still love me?" We need to have the courage to say to God, "I am what I am. I am what you have made me. Is that enough? Do you still love me?"

We find the answer in the small miracles of life whenever we stumble across them. Surely Susan did. And just as surely, so did the family that feasted on—and was healed by—pot roast that wonderful night.

Yet when people talk of healing, they most often mean a physical healing, a miracle of health. Miracles come in many varieties. There are some healings that are physical, some that are emotional, others that heal the soul and spirit. These are experiences that even science cannot understand, let alone explain. The wisest of human healers accept such things. Cancers go away, illnesses are healed, minds and bodies and spirits are restored. How these events are accomplished can be debated. But as when God manifests himself even in an unexpected check at the post office, they are events better to be simply accepted.

Most of what we call miracles are born out of the relationship between God and his people. It's a relationship that calls for our involvement and our commitment.

> "When you enter a town and are welcomed, eat what is set before you. Heal the sick who are there and tell them, 'The kingdom of God is near you.'" (LUKE 10:8–9)

Unforgettable Christmas: One Man's Story

My son, who had not lived at home for more than a year, arrived at our house one day looking weak and feeling poorly. His skin was yellowish, so my wife and I immediately arranged to take him to our family doctor.

The physician took one look and sent him right to the hospital. The next morning, we learned just how serious it was: hepatitis B, an often fatal liver disease. He'd been transferred to an isolation room. Before they would even let me in to see him, the doctor warned that I should prepare myself for the worst.

After I put on a mask, head cover, gown, and gloves, I was finally brought to him. It was ghastly. My son was in bed, tied to the corners hand and foot to keep him from thrashing around. There were IVs and catheters all over the place, bags filled with bloody urine. The walls and ceiling were splattered with blood. He'd been bleeding from his teeth and would spit the blood with such force that it was all over everything. It took doctors and nurses days to get the bleeding under control, but my son was still unable to communicate; he seemed as if he were in a different world. My wife and I spent most of every day at his side. We would pray in the room and in the hospital chapel.

One afternoon, we were there when a nurse came and checked him over. Quickly she phoned a resident specialist, who arrived minutes later with other physicians. They asked us to leave, since our son's vital signs were plummeting. He was not likely to make it through the night, they said.

My wife and I began our vigil about six p.m. that night, both praying mightily but fearing what the doctors had said was inevitable. Two hours later a group came through the hospital corridors singing Christmas songs. I remember thinking to myself, *This certainly will be a Christmas we won't forget.* About eleven p.m., while we continued our prayer vigil, a nurse came out and gently suggested that we go home. There had been no change, and our son's dying could drag on for several more hours. She promised to call as soon as things worsened.

We said our last prayers and perhaps our last good-byes as we went silently to our son's bedside, where we touched him on his forehead, lips, and chest. Then I placed my hands on his abdomen, over his liver, and prayed again. We left.

There were no calls during the night. But the next morning, as we hurried through breakfast to get back to the hospital, the phone rang. I asked my wife to get it.

I heard her answer and feared the worst. Then I listened as she said, "He is? . . . He what? . . . He is?!" Each word was more joyous than the last. She turned to me and said, "He's awake, he's sitting up, he's trying to eat, and he's trying to talk."

Our prayers had been answered. Our son remained in the hospital for several more weeks, then he came home. I have come to believe that I was God's instrument and that this was a miracle.

—*Neil, Lake George, New York*

A Little Help from Above

There have been many miracles, but this one stands out, because it's among the first I ever witnessed. I was a home-health nurse and newly baptized in the Holy Spirit. Even so, I was much more of a doubting Thomas than a bold evangelizer.

One weekend, I was asked to visit a woman who had had abdominal surgery that was not healing properly. As soon as I got there, I could see that her belly was a disaster area, full of boils and draining wounds. She was living in a low-income apartment and was lying on a sofa bed when I showed up at her door. To spare my back from aching later, I knelt on the floor to change her dressings. As I did, it occurred to me to pray for her healing, which I did very quietly to myself.

As I cleansed the wound, I noticed a picture of Jesus by her bedside. She saw me looking and confessed, "Honey, I've been a bad girl. I was a prostitute for many years, and now look at me. A mess." She wept quietly as I held her hand.

That evening, I told friends at a prayer meeting that I had come across a situation that needed a lot of prayer. A group of us got together and prayed for my patient. The following day I returned and told her, "Gloria, I prayed for you last night. How did you do?"

She smiled and answered, "Well, take a look."

Removing the dressing, I saw that the boils had drained and she was beginning to heal. I looked from her belly to her eyes and back again in amazement. She began to weep. Then she told me more of her story, about how she had been raised as a Christian but then let her faith go by the wayside.

Gloria continued to heal, and a few days later when he visited her for a checkup, even the physician who performed the surgery was surprised at her progress. The incisions had all drained and the normal healing process was happening, but at an extremely accelerated rate. He asked what happened. "Well," she said to the surgeon, "you and the other doctors did your best, but my nurse got us a little special help." And she pointed to heaven.

In three days, healing that normally takes three or four weeks was complete. Gloria returned to her church that week. And I learned that God can use doubters as well as seasoned healers in his work.

—*Mary, RN, Portland, Oregon*

Miracle from the Horse's Mouth

Grandmother Evelyn is ninety-five. She's been living with me and has passed down many things to us, not the least of which is her small miracle. Best of all, we've had the opportunity to hear it right from her.

When Evelyn was born, one side of her body was smaller than the other. Her family noticed it soon after birth, and as she grew she began to have convulsions. As often as five times a day, she would topple to the ground and lie there dazed for several minutes. Naturally, she was very embarrassed by this, and her family was careful where she went. Someone always stayed with her to make sure she didn't get hurt.

When Evelyn was only nine, her mother (my great-grandmother) became very ill after the birth of her last child. The doctor and her family knew there was no hope. She asked her children to gather around her for a last visit, and each went to the bedside, one by one. My grandmother remembers as though it were yesterday. She says her mother called her and said, "Le Cit (a pet name meaning "little one" in French), I cannot take you with me where I am going. But from this day forward, you will never again have a seizure."

And she never has.

It is amazing how clearly she remembers the buggy ride to the house that day and how the whole marvelous event took place. Even today she remains a very faithful person. Sometimes stories like these become family legends, but I'm fortunate that my children have had the opportunity to hear this miracle from their grandmother herself.

—*Janet, Herkimer, New York*

I Had Made My Peace . . .

My small miracle—if you can call it that—is that I'm alive.

In 1982 at my oldest son's graduation, I fell ill. The emergency room diagnosis was an inflammation of the intestine. It was a bad case and I was hospitalized. However, during all the routine testing, doctors found a worse problem: I had a large ovarian tumor. They operated immediately. What the surgery uncovered was disheartening. The tumor not only was malignant but had "splashed" into my colon, spreading the cancer.

There was too much of it; the surgeon couldn't get it all. The operating team closed me back up and ordered chemotherapy but told me I had less than a year to live.

In the fall of that same year, after a few rounds of chemo, I returned to the hospital prepared to hear more bad news. Doctors inserted a scope to check the progress of the disease. Amazingly, they found none. Unconvinced by what the scope showed, they reopened my incision for a better look. The cancer was gone. "Impossible," the doctor said to me. That was twelve years ago.

After the first, terrible diagnosis, I had made my peace with life and with God. I was prepared to die. I'd even planned my funeral. I have considered these to be my "bonus years," and have such joy at the goodness of God. The power of prayer and the goodness of God can be overwhelming.

—*Lorene, Champaign, Illinois*

Grandma Couldn't Read, but Could She Pray!

Small miracle? There's been one in our family for years. My mother's mother—my grandmother—was a tiny French-Canadian woman who spoke more French than English. I never could understand her; she would start out speaking in English, but it wasn't long before everything came out in French.

Grandma was illiterate; she could neither read nor write. My mother's daily job was to read the newspaper to her. There was one thing Grandma could do, and that was pray. Oh, how she did pray! I remember, as a young girl, spending the night with her. After tucking me in, she would kneel beside the bed and pray for at least two hours. This was a nightly occurrence; it was something her own mother had taught her to do.

When my mother was eight, her twelve-year-old sister, Florence, became ill with leukemia. More than once I heard my mother speak of the night Florence died, screaming as she hemorrhaged to the end. In 1907 there wasn't anything that could be done to combat this dreaded childhood disease.

Not long after Florence's death, mother's younger sister Eva showed all the same signs of leukemia. When Grandma took Aunt Eva to the doctor, the diagnosis was the same. There was no treatment; just take her home and make her comfortable until she too died.

But Grandma couldn't accept the advice to do nothing. With her strong faith, she ended up taking little Eva by train to a church in Canada famed as a place where healings happened. Even as Grandma knelt in the church to pray for her, Eva suffered a terrible nosebleed. Grandma quickly found one of the clergy and insisted he pray for Eva. The priest prayed but gave Grandma no encouragement, claiming he had no such healing power. But Eva's nosebleed stopped, and all her symptoms of leukemia disappeared.

Today Aunt Eva is eighty-six and is truly a living miracle—healed, I believe, because of her mother's great faith.

—*Ann, Schuylerville, New York*

Not All Healings Are Cures

The "small miracle" we encountered was at the death of our thirty-nine-year-old son from complications of the AIDS virus. Stephen's brother, sister, and I were at his bedside. We prayed for him, and with him, constantly during his last hours with us. We would say the Lord's Prayer over and over.

All the while, Stephen lay dying on a cooling blanket, since his fever had spiked so high. He was on oxygen to help his breathing. In the moments when we were silent, we became aware that the hospital room came alive with its own life. It was full of sounds, medical sounds. The oxygen tank and breathing apparatus made a hissing. The blanket, as it worked to remain cool against Stephen, made a soft click, click, click … Other normal hospital sounds echoed hollowly in the background.

The Lord came to get Stephen as we sat with him. It was as if he picked up my son and carried him off. As Stephen took his final breath, everything around us went silent and peaceful. The oxygen ceased hissing. The blanket stopped its click, click, click … All the sounds were muted.

I felt the presence of God in the room. I really did. I asked my daughter and son if they too sensed it. "Yes," they both said. It was a miracle like I have never felt before, and very hard to put into words. It felt good. It felt as though he were there. And when the sense was gone, the machines began hissing and click, click, clicking again.

But Stephen was not there. He was with God.

—*Ruth, DeKalb, Illinois*

Going Home for Christmas

The yellowed newspaper clipping says it all: "There are no miracles these days, the sages say, but it will be hard to convince little Rita Wanchisen, the seven-year-old Niagara Falls girl who is going home from Memorial Hospital to spend a merry Christmas with her family."

That article appeared in the *Niagara Falls Gazette*, Niagara Falls, New York, on December 18, 1945, two months after I was brutally injured when struck by an automobile. The accident "fractured her skull like an eggshell, broke her left leg, and caused grievous internal injuries," reported the newspaper. Doctors gave me up for dead but still tried to keep me alive. One of the specialists told my parents at the time, "I wish you luck."

And even if I lived, they said, I would surely never walk again. Small miracle? You bet! I don't even limp. And I went home on Christmas Eve.

—*Rita, Passaic, New Jersey*

The Miracle of the Chapel

I was struck down with a severe heart attack a few years ago. It was so bad that my local hospital in central Illinois evacuated me by helicopter ambulance to a major medical center outside Chicago.

About a week after the heart attack, I was hit by a second major problem, a paralytic stroke affecting my right side. Since I'd had several smaller cardiac problems, including bypass surgery, I was always prepared for another heart attack. But the stroke came with no warning.

In fact, it wasn't until the doctors walked in the room one day and noticed how I was acting that I understood. "You've had a stroke," they said. But physicians assured me that I would receive therapy and would be well cared for.

I'm afraid I wasn't a very good patient. I'd had a brother who was paralyzed from polio for seventy years. I remembered what that was like for him; I couldn't handle it. I told the doctors to just let me alone, let me die.

In the usual way of doctors, they ignored my plea.

Later that day, on the way to my first therapy session, the attendant wheeled me past the chapel. As he did, my paralyzed arm moved. I shouted, "Oh my God!" and the attendant turned to ask if he had bumped me. I said, "No," and then pointed out where we were, just outside the chapel. I said to him, "I have a friend in there, you know."

But this miracle isn't quite over.

At the therapy room, the doctors examined me and couldn't find anything wrong, at least in terms of the stroke. Doctors and nurses alike were impressed by this and called it a "God-given miracle."

Ever since, I've had only a minimum of problems; I'm just a little slow. Of course, at the age of eighty, that's not too bad, is it?

—*Roland, Peru, Illinois*

Hospital Visit Ends Fear

This is a true story about my younger brother Patrick. I am the oldest of six children, and even now, thirty years later, I remember it well.

How is it possible for a terrified five-year-old boy and a despairing mother and father to find peace and hope? Well, God does indeed work in strange and wonderful ways.

Patrick, age five, was nearing the end of his life after many months of suffering from a mysterious kidney disease. During the six months he was hospitalized, we five brothers and sisters missed his easygoing personality. We kept up with Patrick through home movies taken by Mom and Dad. Each series of pictures, however, showed his body shrinking little by little. He looked pale, weak, and thin. But always he was smiling and waving.

As a last resort, doctors suggested surgery. His disease was life-threatening, and an operation offered a slim chance for an improvement in the quality of his life. But the surgical technique was new and risky in those days, and he might not make it through. Indeed, he might not even live to make it to the operating room.

The decision was made to go ahead with the operation. Mom and Dad spoke to Patrick. They all cried. Patrick was scared; he didn't want to leave his parents. He didn't want to die. As the hours approaching the procedure clicked by, Patrick's understandable fear turned into terror. He clung to his mother with unbelievable strength. They both cried until there were no more tears left. It took a sedative before he was able to slip into sleep. Only then did he ease his grip on her so she could leave. I doubt if she slept that night.

Mom had to be back at the hospital early the next morning for final preparations for the surgery. With all the fear and hopelessness of the night before still clinging to her, Mother made the trip back to Patrick's hospital room; she wanted to be there when he woke up.

But as she pushed open the door, she saw the happiest, most exuberant child she'd ever seen. Patrick was sitting up straight and strong in his bed and enthusiastically waved her to come closer.

"Mom!" he shouted. "I'm not afraid anymore!" He pressed his little hands to his thin chest, saying, "Jesus came to see me last night. He was dressed in golden-white robes. He held his arms out for me and said I shouldn't worry; the surgery was going to be okay. He said he'd take care of me." Mom wiped the tears from her own eyes as she hugged him. A five-year-old boy who had listened to Jesus comforted his exhausted mother.

Well, you can probably figure out the rest of this story. Patrick not only survived the surgery but grew to be strong and intelligent. He was captain of his high school football team, served as a page in the Commonwealth of Virginia House of Representatives, graduated from college, and has two children of his own now.

—*Maribeth, Deer Park, Texas*

Dairy Farm Depression

I'd like to tell you about one of the small miracles God has performed in my life. I'm a mother of seven, married forty years (that's a miracle, but not the one I'm telling now), and have lived on this same dairy farm in Wisconsin for over thirty-eight years.

A few years ago my youngest son experienced terrible depression that hit him so hard and so suddenly that it almost destroyed him. One night in mid-February, as the rest of the family still living at home was sitting around the dinner table, he phoned. Our daughter answered and listened to Jim as he sobbed and said he wanted to die.

We hadn't seen him for about a week and never knew he was feeling so badly. Of course I immediately went to his home, where he lives alone, and found him lying on the floor, wrapped in a blanket. He hadn't eaten for days.

He's a dairy farmer, too—only about thirty cows—but it had gotten so bad, he couldn't milk them. The family got together and handled the chores around his place. But that didn't begin to take care of Jim. I tried talking to him, but he kept saying that he had nothing to live for and wanted to die. I told him, as best I could, how much God loved him and that he shouldn't give up on something as precious and tremendous as life. I pleaded, I begged, I cried. Nothing helped.

I phoned several professionals but could get no help. Finally, in desperation, I called a cousin in a faraway state. This is a truly Christian woman, a hospital nurse for twenty-three years and someone who believes deeply in the power of prayer and in miracles. She listened as I tearfully cried out my story. She knew that I was in so much need of help at that very moment. She told me how to claim Jim for God, how to rebuke the evil that had taken him, how to pray for him, and how to mark him with the sign of the cross.

I did just as she told me. All the while, my hurting son just lay there. I even lit a candle and quietly hummed a favorite little hymn—"Every day with Jesus is a little better than the day before. . . ." And I was crying at the same time.

After about fifteen minutes of prayer, my son, whom I love so dearly, got up from where he had lain for more than a week. He put on his winter coat and boots and went out the door. I quickly realized that he was headed to the barn for his evening chores. From that moment on, he got better.

It was a miracle, because he had lost hope and faith and the desire to go on in life.

—Betty, Rice Lake, Wisconsin

A Vacation Miracle

I am a history buff, with a particular interest in the Civil War. As such, our family vacations often center around visits to historical sights. In July 1989 we visited the Gettysburg National Battlefield in Pennsylvania, where one of the bloodiest and most decisive conflicts of the Civil War raged. It was also where, family records say, my uncle was wounded on July 2, 1863.

While my daughters and I tramped through the areas with names rich in history and lore—Pickett's Charge, the High Water Mark, and Little Round Top—my wife, Marilyn, remained in our car. A severe arthritic, she was unable to do much walking, because of the pain in her knees and feet.

After more than two days soaking up the history of Gettysburg, we drove to Sharpsburg, Maryland, and the famed Antietam Battlefield. On the way, we passed through Emmetsburg, Maryland, and spotted a very large golden statue perched on a hillside. Our youngest daughter was entranced and wanted to stop, but I refused. We had, I told them, only enough time to visit Antietam.

There, as at Gettysburg, the girls and I walked the battlefield drinking in the history familiar to everyone who's studied the Civil War—the sunken road, the Dunker Church, Miller's cornfield. Just being there made the history come alive for us. Again Marilyn sat in the car.

As we drove back, retracing our steps through Emmetsburg, we again passed the statue. And again our daughter asked to stop. I refused, saying it was almost time for dinner. But she insisted and I reluctantly gave in.

Driving up, we learned that the statue is at the site of the grotto where Saint Elizabeth Ann Seton first taught classes before establishing the first Catholic school in the U.S. The statue was in honor of Mary. It was fascinating, but soon it grew too dark to see all we wanted. We rearranged our schedule and went back the following morning.

During the tour, we stopped at a church on the grounds. Inside, I prayed that some of the pain Marilyn was experiencing would be relieved, at least enough for her to partially enjoy the remainder of our vacation. We left the church and returned to the grotto. I parked as closely as I could to the rest rooms so Marilyn could get to them. When she got out of the car and started down the two steps leading to the facilities, both knees gave audible "snaps," and she would have fallen had the girls not caught her.

But when she got up, the arthritic pain was gone; that was the last such pain she has experienced. From that moment on, Marilyn has been free to dance, climb stairs, walk for exercise, and enjoy her family. She even climbs to mountaintop shrines in our home state.

—*Ken, Security, Colorado*

The Healing Power of Love

This is a story of healing and insight that took place in Cypress, California, more than five years ago. I still treasure it as the first time in my life that I really felt loved.

I am an adult survivor of emotional and psychological abuse as a child. It was for that pain in my life that I was in therapy at the time. I had joined my church choir as a sort of support group, and a fellow choir member had invited both my brother and me to a service at the church.

But as we drove up to the church where the service was being held, I noticed wonderingly that the stars seemed to be shining exceptionally bright that night. Inside, I sat by another choir member and her husband and listened as the mission got under way. The stars were only the beginning; the aura of the place was so peaceful.

I glanced back over my shoulder at the rest of the congregation. I saw a young couple relaxed and leaning against each other as the speaker went on. I really felt the presence of God.

Our choir director was in the pulpit and looked down over the congregation. I saw him and he gave me the most beautiful smile. I felt so loved. I had to look away, since it hasn't been easy as an adult survivor of childhood abuse. But this was truly the first time I had really felt loved.

—*Susan, Los Alamitos, California*

A Parent's Nightmare

My daughter Meghan was in the backseat of a car driven by one of her friends when a car speeding the other way struck them head-on.

Meghan wasn't wearing a seat belt. When rescue workers arrived, they found her in the front seat, head rammed through the steering wheel. She was evacuated by helicopter to the University of Michigan Hospital in Ann Arbor.

We rushed to the hospital, fearing the worst. But what we encountered was even more frightening. She was in critical condition with multiple injuries. The most severe was what is termed a "closed-head injury." She was on life support, and we were warned that she had a ten percent likelihood of survival. And if she beat those terrible odds and lived, she would forever be a very different person than the one who left our dinner table that night.

Meghan remained in a coma for six weeks. When she awoke, we realized that through the grace of God and the efforts of a great medical team, we were rewarded with the return of a family member who, in some ways, is even more wonderful than she was before the accident.

During the initial part of those six weeks, I cannot describe the negative emotions and feelings I had as a father. I told the doctor that if she should live, I wanted the hospital to do everything it could to ensure that she could not feel the tremendous pain her body was certainly experiencing.

There are no words to describe how a parent can feel when they hear that the life of their child is in jeopardy. Yet as I look back on that moment, I recall that I was very controlled about the decision-making process. That's because the faith and strength that comes from God during this kind of crisis is unbelievable.

The first few days were touch and go as the family waited, prayed, and watched the medical team work relentlessly. Our hopes for Meghan's survival went up and down and up and down as crisis after crisis came and passed.

Ten months after the accident, we realized what a miracle we have been blessed with. Meghan participated in her high school graduation and was even presented with the "Against All Odds" award.

And there's more.

Meghan is attending college and has her mind set on a career in occupational therapy, a field that will give her the opportunity to direct the rehabilitation of others who have also experienced severe problems in life. Meghan's own story allows her to provide her patients with an understanding of their struggle that will motivate them toward recovery.

As her father, I thank God every day that I have been given the opportunity to witness this very special miracle.

—*Mike, Barrington, Illinois*

Another Christmas Miracle

God is alive and well! This is one of the moments when he touched my life.

When my daughter Sheila was born a month before Christmas 1951, there was a very small growth between the inside of her eye and the bridge of her nose. I didn't think too much about it until a nurse suggested I take her to an eye specialist.

The specialist told her father and me simply to massage the spot gently a couple of times each day. But after a few days of this, we became very alarmed, because the lump had gotten bigger. Of course, he told us to stop the massage, but it didn't stop the lump. It just grew and grew.

The doctor admitted he was puzzled. It was not, as he once thought, a clogged tear duct, since she had no problem crying. The lump now began turning black and blue as it grew up onto her forehead, completely closing one eye.

On the day before Christmas, we learned that she would have to have surgery immediately after the holiday. Surgery on this tiny month-old girl! This was very frightening to us, and all Christmas Day we prayed and prayed that surgery would not be necessary.

Early the next morning, December 26, I lifted our daughter out of her crib. As soon as I saw Sheila's face, I cried out for her father to come: it was completely normal. There was no lump, no discoloration, and her eyes were both wide open. What a beautiful sight.

We took her back to the doctor, but he could only say, "I have no explanation for this. It's truly amazing." But I have an explanation: God heard us in our time of need and gave us a Christmas miracle.

—*Eleanor, Joliet, Illinois*

A Miracle Mission

You may call them "small" miracles if you want. But I see them as "big," because I had to overcome momentous obstacles but never doubted God would help me.

A little background is always in order.

My mother died of cancer when I was eight, an only child. I had long dreamed of being part of a larger family, with brothers and sisters, but it would not happen. After I married, my husband and I adopted a little boy when it seemed as though we would not be able to have children.

Our life was so joyful until one hot summer day in 1972. My husband, Fred, a New York City police officer, was shot during a narcotics raid. Police rushed me to St. Luke's Hospital in a patrol car. When I saw then–New York mayor John Lindsay and then–police commissioner Patrick Murphy waiting for me, I feared the worst.

But the miracle—the first one—was that the bullet passed through him without hitting anything major. A large scar on his abdomen is the only reminder.

Miracle number two came with the adoption of our second child. As part of that process, we had to have complete physicals, and my husband tested positive for TB. I was devastated, fearing now we would never be allowed to adopt that child. But since my husband was otherwise healthy and the disease was not active, he was treated. We could keep our darling baby girl. She's sixteen now, a talented musician, songwriter, and artist.

The best miracle of all, however, was yet to come.

A few years ago I had a routine mammography. It saved my life, showing a suspicious area. A further examination caught the cancer in an early stage. It was a confusing time, one of many choices and options. At the famed Sloan-Kettering Hospital, an innovative young surgeon did not believe I needed chemo or radiation. I trusted his judgment and put my faith in God.

You see, I had come full circle. When my mother died of cancer so many years before, I had made a silent vow that I would somehow become instrumental in finding a cure for that terrible disease. I didn't want anyone else to experience loneliness and the overwhelming sense of loss that I experienced as a child without a mother.

Because of that, I was drawn into registered nursing. Seeing the suffering of my terminally ill patients compounded my desire to "make a difference." In 1985 I had begun my own private research in my community on Long Island. I was concerned (though "driven" would probably be a better word) about the connection between cancer and environmental pollution. At this point in time, not many people cared to make that connection.

My nursing education and experience trained me to be an observer. And I really cared about our community, particularly the children. It had been a lonely pursuit.

All of this was certainly flashing through my mind that day as I waited in the hospital for my own cancer biopsy, because that day I received a letter from a local legislator that the environmental study of my Holbrook, New York, community had been approved in Albany.

Since then, I have become involved with breast cancer advocacy. I have become a health advocate, bringing up-to-date information to my community. I'm part of an organization that, in conjunction with the National Cancer Institute, is conducting a five-year breast cancer project, the largest study ever undertaken. There will be input from major hospitals and universities.

All this has come about in large measure because of the activism on the part of women on Long Island. The director of the department of preventative medicine at Stony Brook (New York) Hospital said he believes that a cure for the disease of breast cancer will be found here. And more and more, people are recognizing that there is indeed an environmental connection to cancers. I truly believe this is being accomplished through God's infinite grace and wisdom.

—*Mary, Holbrook, New York*

A Montreal Miracle

My roots—and my family's—go deep into Ontario, Canada. My great-great-grandfather built the first wooden Catholic church in Goderich, near the Lake Huron shoreline, in 1833. My education was cut short, while I was still in high school, so that I could help run the family fuel business. I still do.

While I have always considered myself to be a rather unemotional man, my faith has become much deeper in recent years. It was through friends from our church that I first heard the story of Brother Andre.

Brother Andre was a monk who lived more than one hundred years ago in Montreal, Canada. There have been many stories of God's healing surrounding him. I know this; I am one of those stories.

During a checkup at a local hospital, a colonoscopy revealed that I was full of polyps. It was so bad, in fact, that I lowered my eyes, trying to pretend that the awful mess on the screen was not inside me. Doctors made arrangements to have my lower bowel removed and a permanent colostomy placed in my upper intestine. This would be very high-risk surgery for me, and I began to get my affairs in order.

The more I heard the stories of this Brother Andre, the more I agonized whether to visit his city and the church where he had lived. I reflected that God answered prayers in many ways and that if I did not go now—when I felt God's urgings—I'd regret it for the rest of my life.

I decided to go. When my brother-in-law and I arrived, we discovered the church quiet and empty. We wandered through the grounds until we found the general office. When I told them I was making a pilgrimage of sorts, they arranged for us to stay on the property. I was thrilled. I had heard remarkable tales of people who had been healed by God after such a visit. We spent much time in prayer and returned home the following day.

A few weeks later at London University Hospital, London, Ontario, I had the routine preoperative tests. I watched apprehensively as the surgeon assigned to the case did another colonoscopy to check out targets for the operation. This time, in wide-eyed wonder, I listened as he told me my condition didn't seem as bad as he expected from the first doctor's diagnosis. He said he could remove the few polyps he saw with a fiber-optic colonoscope, and the high-risk surgery I was facing would not be necessary.

The packed clusters of polyps I had seen just a few months before were gone. I told the surgeon that I'd had some help from God, but I don't think he was impressed. Still, he set up a full double-contrast barium X-ray and ultrasound exam to confirm his findings.

As I said, I consider myself to be rather unemotional and had been prepared for the worst. I was thankful for the news so far but awaited the further, definitive test results. At last the surgeon came in and told me there were no polyps left—none. They were gone, a miracle indeed.

As we left the hospital, my daughter, who is a nurse, said, "Dad, not many people get good news in this place." It was then that the enormity of my relief finally sank in, and I actually trembled and shed tears of thanks.

—*Grant, Lucknow, Ontario, Canada*

God Who Heals

Touch my mind, my body.
Touch my soul, my heart.
You have the way to make me whole, to restore me.
Love me into that wholeness, Lord.
Fill me with the Spirit who heals.
Most of all, Lord,
> give me the ability to recognize, in you, the way to end my brokenness.

Help me to trust
> that in my growing relationship with you, I will be healed.

Amen.

Four

🔊

Miracles on the Battlefield

For any kid in kindergarten, life is an adventure story, with one exciting chapter following another. That's because children, full of wonder and wide-eyed enthusiasm, are experience sponges. Throw something at them and they'll absorb it, and it will bounce around inside them until it has to burst out and be told.

Ask a kindergartner what he did at school that day. The response is likely to be something like this: "What did I do? Wow, there was coloring and letters and someone brought in a pet and we visited the firehouse and the kid next to me threw up at lunch and I lost my book bag and on the way home I fell into a mud puddle."

Whew. All those experiences just bubble up because, frankly, they cannot be contained. Try it and you just explode. There's just too much excitement. Sometimes those of us who call ourselves adults forget to become that excited over the stories of our lives. We allow ourselves to be underwhelmed by it all. There's a T-shirt on the market these days that sums up our blasé approach to the wonders of the world: "Been there. Done that. Bought the shirt."

Which, of course, is too bad. Because we live in a world in which there are compelling things, stories that deserve to burst out and be told because they cannot be contained.

Lots of those stories are about faith. They are the stories of a God who—like the wonder of a child—cannot be contained. The excitement of those who tell them is so genuine and so real—and so compelling—that we have to listen and believe.

To be compelling, you have to be real. The faith tales of the early church—with its almost larger-than-life figures of Paul and Peter and Barnabas and Stephen—are certainly compelling. It was bold and compelling faith that spread the word of early Christianity. These are stories that still populate our Bibles and other literature of faith.

> As Paul and Barnabas were leaving the synagogue, the people invited them to speak further about these things on the next Sabbath. . . .
>
> On the next Sabbath almost the whole city gathered to hear the word of the Lord. When the Jews saw the crowds, they were filled with jealousy and talked abusively against what Paul was saying.
>
> Then Paul and Barnabas answered them boldly: "We had to speak the word of God to you first. Since you reject it and do not consider yourselves worthy of eternal life, we now turn to the Gentiles. For this is what the Lord has commanded us:
>
> "'I have made you a light for the Gentiles,
>   that you may bring salvation to the ends of the earth.'"(ACTS 13: 42, 44–47)

But that was then and this is now. We modern-day Christians don't always think of our faith as either bold or compelling. We don't often hear bold or compelling stories. Sometimes we just sort of go along.

So let me tell you a story that I think is a compelling one. And bold. It happened a long way from kindergarten—as far as from the playground to the battleground.

The man who told me this story is named Bill Abbott. He hails from New York and still, decades later, makes his home on Long Island. Abbott's New York roots figure prominently in this real-life story of faith and effort and prayer and miracle. When he relates the tale, the power of his excitement is infectious. It's a story of World War II, and even half a century later it's still bubbling out. It cannot be contained.

The year was 1944. World War II was at its height. Europe was in flames, and the Allies had begun to slowly wrest back the continent from Hitler. In the Pacific, GIs were slogging from island to island, leaving in their wake the Stars and Stripes but also wounded and dead comrades. The seas were speckled with ships and battles and heroes.

Abbott was a young midshipman in training to be a naval officer. The classes weren't the problem; swimming was. "I couldn't swim," he said. "Not a stroke. And the U.S. Navy frowned upon nonswimmers and absolutely refused to commission anyone who couldn't swim."

He said there were instructors, of course, and they were good. "But the final exam was so rigorous that it was very unlikely that someone like me—unable to even take my foot from the bottom—could be raised to the necessary skill level in four short months. My only hope was prayer."

So each morning before his classes, Abbott was at the academy chapel, asking prayerfully for God's help at the pool during his unavoidable trial by water.

He had delayed the test as long as possible. But the day before graduation, he and another student with the same problem were ordered to the pool. They sat there in regulation blue swimming trunks, recognizing that no matter what else happened, this would be the single test that would determine the course their lives would take. It sounds too much like a cliché, but for these two aspiring naval officers, that day it was literally sink or swim.

The testing officer, a lieutenant, called the other cadet first. With an almost visible sense of resignation, he jumped into the chilly water. Despite struggling greatly, he failed. The testing officer told him to report to the academic office. He was through.

It was Abbott's turn. He remembers crossing the slippery tile around the edge of the pool and launching himself off toward the other end. With every stroke came a prayer, and quickly he was praying as hard as he was flailing away at the water. But it was no use. The water seemed to hold him back; the far end of the pool was still far away—too far away.

Finally—his God and his effort notwithstanding—it was over. Halfway through, he couldn't go on. He reached out and grasped the side of the pool, an action by which he automatically disqualified himself. His prayers had failed.

Abbott caught his breath briefly at the edge, then pulled himself out of the pool to report to the testing officer. Certainly, he would quickly follow in the footsteps of the other would-be officer, right out the door. Their conversation went like this:

"Where you from, Abbott?"

"New York, sir."

"I thought so. You sound like New York. Know any cops, Abbott?"

Abbott had three uncles, all New York City policemen. So he said, "Yes, sir."

"What're their names?"

"Tim, Bill, and Ed."

"What's Tim?" the officer asked.

"A detective," Abbott answered.

"He's also one of my best friends," said the lieutenant. "Go back to your section, Abbott, and just make sure you don't fall overboard for the rest of the war."

His prayers were answered—though not as he had expected.

Abbott told me that when he realized afterward what had just happened, he thought, *Had I jumped into the water for the test and swum the distance, maybe my prayers would have worked. Or maybe I would have been able to swim because I was convinced I could. If I had succeeded, it might have been a miracle. Or it might have not been. We'd never know. But I didn't make it. I failed.*

Please note: The testing officer was honest. He didn't say, "You passed." He just sent the young midshipman back to his section. Abbott never heard from him again. "The following day, I graduated with my class and went to sea," he said. "During World War II, there were 385,000 officers in the U.S. Navy. What were the odds that one who was my uncle's best friend would be the one to administer my swimming test on that day? It was a minor miracle, to be sure, but one which confirms the awesome power of prayer."

Bill Abbott has obviously told that story many times in the half-century-plus since. Each time, he's able to pass along the excitement of what was for him an adventure with God—an adventure of prayer—no less than some of those experienced by people named Paul or Barnabas or Titus or Stephen. It was that real. It is certainly as compelling as many Bible stories. Such witness—such evangelism—is a powerful antidote for spiritual boredom. Compelling stories not only keep faith alive but make it flourish.

Abbott may not think of his story as evangelism, but it is. So are other stories of faith we share with one another. There are stories of how God has broken through into lives, how faith has touched people, how the presence of grace has been real and alive and exciting.

One last thing about Bill Abbott's wartime experience with prayer and the miracle of faith. Whenever he tells of his adventure as a midshipman, he said, he makes sure of two things: first, that he never forgets to credit the power of faith; and second, that he tells people that no, he never did fall overboard.

Everyone's heard the cliché "There are no atheists in foxholes." Of course, no cliché is one hundred percent true, and undoubtedly atheists have populated foxholes now and again. But the thrust of the saying is that war brings out in most of us a recognition of our vulnerability, our fragility, our humanity. Maybe it's the sense of desperation, or lack of personal control, war brings that allows—encourages, compels—us to turn to prayer and to seek miracles. Because war is such a frightful experience, it is also fertile ground for miracles to happen. Some of those miracles are grounded in a God who we believe is close. Other miracles may flow from a faith we thought was long forgotten but wasn't.

Home Front

As you will see, this was not a small miracle to me. It was something very much larger.

In 1945, the closing year of World War II, my husband was drafted into the U.S. Army. We had five children at home, all under the age of nine. I begged the draft board, but it was no use. After he left, we were alone. It was a rural area and the nearest telephone was more than a mile away. As you might expect, I was very distraught and cried a lot.

One Sunday afternoon, I stopped at our small church and pleaded to God for help. As I sat there crying before God, I heard a small voice say, "Write. Write a letter to the army chaplain and tell him about your problem."

I didn't know who or where the chaplain was but wrote that letter anyway. I addressed it to Chaplain, Fort Lewis, Tacoma, Washington. I told him about our family and about our need to have a husband and father back home.

My husband, in basic training by this time, didn't know about the letter. A week went by and he received a call that the chaplain wanted to see him. When they met, the chaplain showed my husband the letter I wrote and asked if it was all true. My husband was shocked but said it was. My husband was home by the next week.

We've now been married almost sixty years, and I'll never forget the miracle of 1945. Thanks to God.

—*Dorothy, Rhinelander, Wisconsin*

The Music and the Memory

My brother went to fight in Vietnam. He never came home. It was—and remains—a painful loss to us, his family. When he enlisted in the marines, he told us that his reasons had a lot to do with the lyrics of a song very popular around that time. The song was "Born Free," and the sense of it was that people had to follow wherever they felt the spirit calling them.

The first Christmas after he was killed in battle was very hard. One of our cousins knew it would be a difficult holiday, so he insisted that we share it with him at his home. My brother's song—the one that spelled out, for him, the reasons he had to sign up and go to the war that killed him—was still very popular. Knowing that it was frequently played on radio and understanding how it would affect us, my cousin was careful to dial in a station that advertised twenty-four uninterrupted hours of Christmas music and hymns.

We sat quietly in his living room, listening to carols playing, trying to celebrate the holiday. Suddenly, in the middle of melodies of the hope and joy of Christ's birth, the haunting notes of "Born Free" began to flow from the radio. My cousin leaped from his chair to turn it off, change the station, or something—just to stop the song. But it was too late. We had already dissolved into sobs.

Yet the tears of grief mixed with tears of wonder, because suddenly I understood that my brother's spirit and his memory was still with us.

And always would be. Perhaps it was the combination of memories and music, emotions and Christmas. The veil between heaven and earth may conceal the faces of our loved ones, but it is not always soundproof. That has become even more apparent after more than two decades of reflection. Thank you for letting me share my story, because the more I think of my life, the more miracles I find.

—*Judith, Mount Prospect, Illinois*

A Leap of Faith

After the Allied invasion of Normandy, I was commanding the Fourteenth Hospital Train as it chugged through the darkness of the French countryside. We were following the advancing battlefield and would treat and evacuate wounded GIs. It was a journey we had made—and would make—often during the intense fighting to rescue the continent from Hitler.

Suddenly the train ground to a halt in the black night, its steel wheels squealing on the rails. The commanding officer of the entire train unit ordered me to find out what was holding up our progress to the front. We were needed there, and a delay could prove costly. Ordinarily this would have meant for me simply to jump off the English-built railcar we normally used and walk to the head of the train and talk to the engineer.

But on this trip, the English car we had brought across as part of the invasion had developed a hot box on one of the wheels. It had to be replaced by a French-built car of a much different design. Because of the unfamiliar car, I briefly paused to glance outside before stepping to the rocky railbed. I was shocked to see that we had stopped not on a stretch of normal track but on a high trestle. Looking down, instead of solid ground, all I could see were a few pinpoints of light twinkling in the gloom far below.

Had I jumped in my usual way, I would have tumbled off the bridge into the dark and died. Instead, I stood and clung to the rail of that life-saving French railcar, thanking God.

I returned from the war untouched by the horrors many others suffered. And I always believed that dark night deep in the French countryside was my miracle.

—*Robert, Aurora, Illinois*

A Battlefield Angel

I survived World War II, from the Battle of the Bulge in 1944 to meeting up with the Russians in Germany the following year. I was an infantryman who had come close to being killed many times but came through without a scratch.

Still, I've had a couple of miracles myself. I told my family it must have been their prayers that kept me safe.

During a battle, my company had orders to take and secure an important road junction. We were at our objective when artillery began hitting us. A shell exploded less than ten feet away. I saw the blinding flash but hardly heard it; nor did I feel the great concussion that must have buffeted us all. An artillery shell like that throws out hundreds, perhaps thousands, of tiny, white-hot shards of metal. This shrapnel, along with the concussion, is what kills.

Close as I was to the burst, not a fragment struck me.

The soldier just a few feet away suffered a massive head wound; others were knocked senseless by the blast. I was unscathed. An angel was on my shoulder.

Later in that same campaign, we were battling for high ground when a mortar round struck and killed my radio operator, who was running right alongside me. Once again it must have been my angel, whose voice I clearly heard above the noise of the shooting, telling me to "get the hell out of there."

Strong language for an angel, perhaps, but quite appropriate. Quickly I gave the order to fall back, which we did. We were barely out of range when the area where we had been erupted, with a score or more mortar rounds tearing up the ground in every direction. It would have killed us all.

I could tell lots of miracles about soldiers I served with, too. At our unit's forty-fifth reunion, a fellow soldier confided an incident that had happened to him. He had never told anyone, he said, about the night they were under an enemy artillery attack. Shells were falling all around them, when suddenly he felt a tremendous punch, right in his chest. Then nothing else.

Later when the unit had moved out of range and the shelling had stopped, he took the prayer book his mother had given him from his left shirt pocket to pray. As he flipped it open, a jagged chunk of shrapnel fell out. It had gone halfway through the book instead of through his heart.

I could tell you many more. And years later I still thank God every night and every day.

—*Name withheld, River Falls, Wisconsin*

A Piece of Home in a Pocket

The letter that arrived in our rural Oregon mailbox was addressed to me. It was from Uncle Sam, ordering me into the army. My two older brothers were already fighting in World War II. Now it was my turn.

I had thirty days to report. Once I left, my father would be left to run our 175-acre farm, with only my youngest brother and four sisters to help. I knew this concerned my father, though he never spoke of it. I knew just how much he missed his sons.

A week before I was to leave for the base—I remember the evening well—my mother asked me to sit with her while the family prayed. She reached into her sewing basket and pulled out a tiny leather folder. Inside was a small religious symbol she had lovingly crocheted. She asked me to carry this while serving my country.

I reported for duty, was trained in the art of warfare and shipped out to the hellhole called Okinawa. This island in the Pacific became the scene of some of the fiercest fighting in the war, against an entrenched and stubborn enemy. As the battle surged around us, the sergeant ordered us to attack. Just eight days after my twenty-first birthday, I was shot twice. The first bullet sent me hobbling toward safety. As I did, the second tore into my chest, passed near my heart, and burst out through my shoulder. The enemy left me for dead.

But I was found by medics and survived. They kept me alive, patched up my wounds, and sent me home. Though I was grievously wounded, my parents were certain my return was due to their prayers— and that small crocheted symbol of their faith.

My recuperation took quite a while. But I was anxious to begin helping with the chores, feel the fresh morning air in my lungs, and be a farmer once again.

Three years later, after a long day in the field, I realized my wallet was missing. It would have been impossible to retrace my many steps that day, so I went through the effort of replacing my ID cards, driver's license, and the rest of those important documents. The following summer, one of my younger sisters stumbled on my wallet in the brush while picking blackberries. Only one thing in the wallet survived a year exposed to the elements: the piece of crocheted yarn my mother made.

Some time later I was baling hay when the machine clanked to a stop for no apparent reason. I was puzzled and hoped a repair wasn't necessary, since the delay would dry out the hay and lose income for the farm. As I peered inside the baler, I discovered my wallet, which had fallen from my pocket. The next slash of the blades would have turned it to mulch. As it was, one corner had been sliced off, though the emblem inside was untouched.

Time and again through the years, this sort of thing has been repeated.

Once I returned from sitting in an auction all day to find my wallet gone. The following week, again at the auction, a man called me by name and handed me my missing wallet. I checked it immediately. The missing two hundred dollars could be replaced, but the bit of crocheting was safe. I hoped the man's conscience was as clear as mine.

Each autumn, after the crops are harvested, the fields are burned off to eliminate insects and disease and prepare the soil for the following spring. One fall as I was walking the fields after the annual burn, I found my wallet lying in a patch of green grass, untouched by the fire that had scorched all around it.

Miraculous acts of God? I think so.

When I was discharged from the army a half century ago, I had five medals on my chest and a patch on my sleeve. Today they lay in a box in some drawer. The small religious symbol with a red-and-pink border my mother crocheted for me so long ago remains in my wallet.

—*Raymond, Portland, Oregon*

The Shouts No One Could Hear

July 1945. The war in Europe was over. The rebuilding had begun. For many of the guys who had fought their way across the continent, it meant going home to families. But not for all of us. The war in the Pacific wasn't over.

Instead, some of us were reassigned to the Eightieth Field Hospital as surgical corpsmen—destination: somewhere in Japan, if the planned invasion became a reality needed to end the war. It was summer

1945. We knew nothing of the atomic bomb that would end the war without us.

Our staging area was in southern France, near Marseilles. We were issued the equipment and clothing we would be expected to need in the final, upcoming campaign. Finally, after more training, we were given some R and R—rest and recreation.

It was a perfect day: warm, some breeze and lots of sunshine. My buddy and I decided to go swimming in the ocean. We gathered our gear and headed to the beach. Walking along, we came upon some flat-bottomed boats like ones we had used for river crossings. We figured we could handle those; we had done so before.

Time just stood still for us. There were no casualties back at the field hospital to worry about, and whatever might happen in the future was far away. One of us would relax in the boat while the other rowed. But suddenly my buddy realized we were caught in a current and were being swept out to sea. In his excitement, trying to get back on course, he snapped our only oar.

Desperately, frantically, we tried to paddle our way back to shore with arms and hands, but it was useless. There was no one in sight, just some onrushing gray clouds and ocean waves. We kept drifting farther and farther out from shore. Once we passed near a buoy and tried to hang on, but it was too rough.

Only heaven could help us. My buddy knelt down in the boat and began crying and praying, because it surely looked hopeless. I tried to be composed and prayed silently, asking for God's help—or something. I was helpless and afraid.

Amazingly, I felt much of what the apostles must have experienced during the storm on the Sea of Galilee, when Jesus was asleep in the back of the boat and they feared for their lives. For some reason I became calm. Then, out of nowhere, I spotted a small motor launch heading toward us through the seas. Frantically I waved.

The launch pulled alongside. Inside was a gentleman dressed in a crisp white uniform of some sort that I didn't recognize. He had two others with him. They shouted that they had heard us calling for help. One of them threw us a line, and they towed us back to the place we had left.

After we dragged the boat up on the shore, I turned to thank them, but they had gone, vanished. Only then did we realize how strange the rescue was. Our shouts could hardly have been heard very far over the rumbling of the waves. And yet we were saved.

And more than that, we weren't shipped out to fight in Japan, because that war too ended. We went home.

—*Alexander, Joliet, Illinois*

Platoon at Pleiku

The village—and the battle that we fought there—was called Pleiku. It happened in 1967. The first miracle was that I survived there. The second is that I continue to survive here.

I was a grunt (soldier) with the U.S. Army's twenty-fifth Infantry Division. And I'll never forget Pleiku. There were ninety men in my company going into the battle. When it was over, only nineteen were left alive. Only eight of the thirty-eight GIs in my platoon survived. I was one, but a Vietcong bullet cut me down, and I lay in the jungle, alone, for more than ten hours, praying and wondering if each minute would be my last. The rifle bullet struck me in the shoulder, cut through to the bone, where it ricocheted downward, passing out through my armpit.

The miracle was that I didn't bleed to death right there. But the way I fell kept my arm close to my body, effectively blocking the wound from bleeding me dry in all those hours. I didn't even suffer from shock. The wound took me out of the war and brought me home. I'm an eighty-percent-disabled Vietnam veteran, but I'm alive.

Being disabled has limited the sort of job I can do. For ten years I labored as a security guard with low pay and no job future or much security. But recently I was hired by a firm that is training me to become a purchasing agent. I now have my own office, and I truly believe this is a miracle job, given me by God.

—*John, Barto, Pennsylvania*

Knock of the Gestapo

Not all the miracles of war are miracles of the battlefield. That's because not all those who do battle are soldiers. Sometimes they are ordinary people. And the miracle is that they can do extraordinary things.

It began when my mother, Dr. Irena Kowalewski-Szretter, was a dentist practicing in Warsaw, Poland. Nazi soldiers had conquered our country. Although she was not directly involved, my mother knew that her dentist's waiting room was secretly being used by the Polish resistance as a place to exchange information. This already dangerous situation was made even more so, because my parents were secretly sheltering a Jewish woman to keep her out of the death camps.

In September 1942, when I was three months old, the soldiers came for Mother. They arrested her and took her to the worst of the Nazi prisons. You can imagine how her arrest affected the rest of her family. But for her it meant interrogations, torture, concentration camp, and almost certain death.

At the prison, she was lined up with other inmates and told to strip. As they stood there naked, the Gestapo officers ordered the women to remove their jewelry and hand it over. Mother took off everything, except for a gold chain with her religious medals attached. As the Gestapo officers were coming down the line collecting the jewelry, she struggled desperately to detach the little silver medal of Saint Teresa of Lisieux from the chain.

As she wrestled with it, one of the officers stood in front of her and demanded, "What are you doing?" She pleaded with him, saying, "I'm trying to detach this little medal from the chain. It's not gold; you really don't need it. Please let me keep it."

With that, the Gestapo man snatched the chain from her hand. He tried to separate the medal himself but failed. Then he pulled, twisted, and tried to break the chain. Though young and strong, the chain defeated him. Suddenly he stopped, looked at my mother, and snarled, "Here, you can keep the whole thing."

At that moment, my mother had an overwhelming sense that God was with her and that she would survive this humiliation. And survive she did, both the interrogations and the beatings. She survived without giving up the information being demanded.

To everyone's astonishment, the Nazis released her. Though she was gravely ill with infectious hepatitis and nearly died, she honored a promise made during her imprisonment. The promise was that if, through a miracle, she survived, she would name her daughter—me— after Saint Teresa. And she did.

Not only my mother but our whole family believe her release was a miracle. She was one of the very few Poles released alive from that infamous prison. Perhaps this was not such a "small" miracle after all.

—*Teresa, Bartlett, Illinois*

જ

Miracles and faithfulness do not go unnoticed. For their faithfulness in sheltering Jews during the Holocaust, Teresa's mother and father were subsequently honored by the government of Israel. They were given medals of honor and are remembered on Yad Vashem, the Avenue of the Righteous, a monument in Jerusalem to the honorable Gentiles who placed selflessness and humanity over personal danger during the Holocaust.

Lord Who Saves

Humankind turns, too often, to force instead of to love.
Yet even in moments of war, in the flashes of battle,
   we can hear the trumpets of God announcing rescue.
Lord, that sense is echoed throughout your word.
"Even though I walk through the valley of the shadow of death,
   I will fear no evil, for you are with me;
   your rod and your staff, they comfort me.
"You prepare a table before me in the presence of my enemies.
   You anoint my head with oil; my cup overflows.
"Surely goodness and love will follow me all the days of my life,
   and I will dwell in the house of the LORD forever".

—PS. 23:4–6

Lord, you are a God of peace and love and comfort,
   not a God of war and hate and anger.
Help us turn to you, even when the shouts of anger and hate
   threaten to drown out your words.
For if we trust, you will save us.
Amen.

Five

❧

Flowers—Bloomin' Miracles

*I*t's no secret. Every kid longs for the day when he or she no longer has to do what they are told to do. You did it; I did it.

Those of us who are parents have endured the toddler's stubborn and emphatic "No!" and the youngster's whining "Why do I hafta . . .?" and the teenager's defiant "You can't make me do nuthin'!" And truth be told, how many of us also long to tell our boss, spouse, even our minister and the cop who stops us for a traffic violation, the same thing?

Of course, the teenager is closest to the truth. Because in the real world—the place where most of us adults spend our days—there is truly very little "must," surrounded by a great deal more "choice." We always have a choice—as long as we are willing to live with the sometimes exceedingly uncomfortable consequences of our actions. Children eventually learn that what they grudgingly believed were unacceptably harsh "orders" and "instruction" were really "direction" and "guidance."

This is not a new thing. Throughout his public ministry, Jesus never forced an action on anyone. It was always presented as a choice, a direction to be followed. Or ignored. Which is what sometimes happened when people met him. It still does.

Deciding what path we take, what direction, whose words and advice we follow, is the stuff of life. Ask James, a middle-aged man from Glen Ellyn, Illinois, who has looked back over the years of his family's history and has come to understand the powerful, fulfilling role of letting God be the guide. This is his story. It's the Miracle of the Yellow Rose.

The adventure takes place in the early 1940s. The woman who would become James's mother had fallen in love with a man who, though a Christian, was not of her family's faith. It was a different time; ecumenism, even between differing denominations, was an uncomfortable thing. And whether to enter into a "mixed" marriage was a big decision.

In love though she was, his mother questioned herself, asking, *Is this man the right one?* She even decided to seek an answer in prayer, asking for a special sign—a yellow rose—if it was God's will that she should marry him.

After visiting her church to pray, she and one of her sisters went downtown to shop. Walking through a large department store, they came upon a long line of women. "What is the line for?" they asked. It turned out that the store was giving away a free flower to each customer. Of course, they joined the line and awaited their turn.

But this tale is about hearing the guidance of a God who sometimes whispers rather than shouts. How—or even whether—we hear the urgings of God depends on many things. And of course, we always have the choice to listen or not. Too often we make our decisions not on what we might believe but on the apparent realities of the moment.

That may be why the story of the rich young man touches such a nerve with us. We've all been there. It's from the Gospel of Matthew.

Now a man came up to Jesus and asked, "Teacher, what good thing must I do to get eternal life?"

"Why do you ask me about what is good?" Jesus replied. "There is only One who is good. If you want to enter life, obey the commandments."

"'Which ones?" the man inquired.

Jesus replied, "'Do not murder, do not commit adultery, do not steal, do not give false testimony, honor your father and mother,' and 'love your neighbor as yourself.'"

"All these I have kept," the young man said. "What do I still lack?"

Jesus answered, "If you want to be perfect, go, sell your possessions and give to the poor, and you will have treasure in heaven. Then come, follow me."

When the young man heard this, he went away sad, because he had great wealth. (MATT. 19:16–22)

The rich young man didn't heed the words of direction and chose to walk in a different direction. The better decision was too hard for him to stomach, so he left. Scripture doesn't relate Jesus' reaction, though it would hardly have been one of flippancy. More likely, given his enduring compassion, the reaction would have been one of sadness. And of permission, since neither guidance nor faith can be imposed; they must be chosen. And we must learn to see, in the world around us, the signs that point the direction for us.

For the young woman waiting for a flower in a long department store line, perplexed about her future, what directions did she hear? And what directions did she heed?

It would be simple—and perhaps even miraculous—to say that at the end of that line, she was handed a yellow rose, a sign of her love and the sign she sought. But that's not what happened. God doesn't always work so transparently.

The line they were in was long, snaking through the store. After a while, a store floorwalker came up to them, saying, "Ladies, perhaps you'd like to stand in that other line over there. I think you'll be served much faster." He pointed across the sales floor to a similar line.

James said, "My mother and her sister moved to the other line. At the end, each received her flower. And yes, it was a yellow rose. My mother could also see what she would have received had she remained in the first line, where they had waited so long: a red rose. The directions had been good ones."

Was this the sign? She wasn't sure, so the prayers continued, asking for something more. This time, after the prayer she returned home. Later there was a knock on her door. It was her boyfriend, bearing a bouquet. Of yellow roses.

No more praying for signs. No more doubt. He proposed; she accepted. There were three sons; one would become a man of God. "The marriage lasted nearly until their fiftieth anniversary, when my father died. Yes, he was the right one," James said.

Letting God be a guide can be frightening. Because it also allows us, should we choose to ignore the signs, to walk away, like the rich young man.

The rest of the miracles in this chapter are also about flowers, often providing a direction in life, a sign from God. Some people might believe that something as beautiful as a flower would, by itself, qualify as a miracle. They'd be right, of course, but most miracles need to involve people in a very special and very intimate way.

The Gardenia of Memory

Something strange happened when my mother was living with us. She was ill and very much in pain. I had bought her a beautiful gardenia plant, loaded with buds and ready to bloom. I hoped it would make her feel better just to be able to look at it and smell its scent.

Though we took very good care of the plant, the buds soon started falling off without blooming. We hurriedly asked the florist for advice and did everything he said. But nothing worked; soon the plant was bare. It had not borne a single blossom, leaving Mother very sad indeed. Though it remained a lush and beautiful plant, it never bloomed.

After we had the plant two years, I told Mother we might as well get rid of it, since nothing was going to happen. She said, "No."

Then she told me to keep the gardenia until after she passed away. That's when it would bloom, she said. She said it would be a sign from God that she was in heaven and freed from her terrible pain. I confess, I didn't put too much hope or trust in my mother's words. But we kept the plant.

Mother died that next June. Three months later—deep into the fall and well past a gardenia's normal blooming time—the plant suddenly burst into full color. It was gorgeous. After blooming profusely, it died, shedding all its leaves. I kept the plant for another year to see if it would come back; it didn't. It seemed to have given its message and all that it had. Its task completed, it died.

To this day, it gives me a good feeling to think about this. It was, for me, a true miracle. Thanks for letting me share this, because when I tell others about it, they give me that look you get when someone doubts you are telling the truth.

But I know. And it has made a difference in my life.

—*Alice, Ontario, Oregon*

A Purple-and-White Message

Many years ago my sister-in-law had given our family a pot of ground cover plants that were supposed to spread over the garden and keep it a nice green—except when they bloomed. Then it was supposed to be full of beautiful purple flowers.

Except that it never bloomed. It never did anything; it just sat there. For years.

My sister-in-law had been ill for a long time and died. A few weeks after we buried her, four blooms appeared on the long-bare plants. Three were purple. One was white. No one in the family said much when we saw the plant. But somehow we knew that she was okay; she was with God. And we understood.

—*Loretta, Medford, New York*

Giving Away a Miracle

I love telling my little miracle. It happened many years ago. A friend and I would frequently go out to lunch and then, if we had the time, do a little shopping. On this particular day, a beautiful sunshiny one, we stopped in a five-and-dime store, where they were selling real roses for ten cents. (I told you this was many years ago.) I bought one and tucked it into my bag.

My friend Mary bought a dozen, and the saleslady carefully wrapped paper around the stems and handed them back to her. As we left the store, we met another friend and stopped to chitchat. That friend couldn't stop admiring Mary's dozen roses, saying repeatedly, "Oh, how beautiful they are."

I kept thinking to myself, *Why doesn't Mary just give her one? She's got a dozen.* But suddenly I found myself reaching into my bag, pulling out my one and only rose, and offering it to Mary's friend. Gratefully accepting the rose, Mary's friend explained that she was out of work and had been praying for a job and a sign that everything would be okay. We talked for a few more minutes and went on our separate ways.

By then, Mary finally realized I had given my only rose, and pulled one from her dozen and handed it to me. "I don't know why I didn't give her one of mine," she said. "I had twelve and you had only one."

I walked back to my office, and Mary took a bus home. Soon I got a call from Mary. She said, "Didn't I give you a rose?" I glanced over my shoulder at the flower sitting there in a glass of water and said, "Of course you did. I'm looking right at it. Why?"

"Well," Mary said, "because I've still got twelve."

Oh, I know people will say the salesclerk made a mistake and really gave her thirteen. So it may be. But months later while taking care of some business, I again ran into Mary's friend—the one to whom I had given the rose that day—who was working in that office.

She beamed at me and said, "This is the job I got the day you gave me the rose."

—*Theresa, Albany, New York*

Picking a Purple Miracle

Two springs ago while living in rural Missouri, my young daughter Catherine and I attended church services together. As a reward to her for behaving in church, we visited a park after returning home.

Not far from the park was a house where we had once lived. As we walked past it, my daughter spotted some purple and yellow crocuses popping up in the lawn of "her old home." Of course she wanted to run into the familiar yard and pick them. I told her no, because someone else lived there now. That seemed to satisfy her, though it was apparent that she was attracted by the purple flowers. That was probably because the only ones we had in our own yard were bright yellow daffodils. They were beautiful, but my daughter was fascinated with the purple ones.

Just a few mornings later the two of us were in our yard picking those daffodils for a spring bouquet. We discovered in the midst of this yard of yellow daffodils two blooming purple and white crocuses.

I was overwhelmed. I told Catherine that her angel heard her when she asked to pick the crocuses and sent us these. She, in the wisdom of a child, smiled and said, "There's one for me and one for you."

—*Carol, Lombard, Illinois*

Praying, Waiting, Thanking

God did indeed give my husband and me a small miracle, a definite moment when we knew that he had touched our lives.

Before we even met, both of us had prayed for guidance to see if God had wanted us to marry again after surviving disastrous relationships. I didn't really think I would remarry but asked God to choose someone, if indeed that was his plan for me. My choices have not always been the best, and I figured God would do a better job.

I also asked for a sign so that I would recognize God's choice for me. The sign I asked for was a single red rose.

Then I met Horace, someone I would not have even considered as a mate. He is black and I am white. And he's several years younger than I am. It was a difficult step for me to pursue a relationship with him at first, and I fought it. But Horace was nice and interesting to know. He is also a man with a powerful faith.

He explains it this way: he prays, thanks God, and then waits. Simple, faithful, expectant.

After we had gotten to know each other a little bit, I told him that I had asked God for a sign for me. Horace said he felt sure that God would tell him. So he prayed and he thanked God and he waited.

One evening, he told me he knew what the sign was. "A single rose," he said. I was stunned. "What color?" I demanded. "Red," he said. Horace later told me he was surprised it was something so simple.

To complete the story, I got my rose and we were married. That was more than four years ago. When the ups and downs of married life come, I remember that God chose us for each other.

—*Pat, Arvada, Colorado*

The Lily That Refused to Die

My sister was expecting her second child. Suddenly a peaceful, summer Sunday morning was shattered by a flurry of phone calls from her home in Atlanta to our parents and then to each of her five brothers and sisters, including me.

Something was wrong, dreadfully wrong, and there was a possibility that either she, the child, or both could die from some unanticipated complications.

Pray? Of course I prayed. Though I concede it was panicky begging at first. Then as the hours passed with no news, good or bad, my prayers in church turned to this:

"God, I beg you to let them both live. Yet I know that you can bring good out of anything, so I ask you to prepare us and help us through this if there is a tragedy to face. And Lord, could I ask a personal favor? This not knowing is unbearable. Somehow, please give me a sign if they are going to be okay."

As I finished the prayer, one of the elderly women who helps take care of our church walked in with a lily blossom in her hand and a puzzled look on her face.

"I don't understand this at all," she said. "This lily was thrown out and has been lying in the grass for more than a week. All the other lily blossoms from the church, whether cuttings or still on the plants, have died." There'd been no rain, and she said that the bloom had been lying in the same place on the grass, sometimes in shade, sometimes in sun.

I too had remembered passing the discarded bloom during the week but assumed it was artificial and left it lying there.

"What's keeping it alive, I wonder?" she said as she handed me the still very fresh blossom.

Immediately I realized that my sister and her baby were going to be fine. A phone call an hour later confirmed it. Of course, the only thing new for me was that I had a niece and not a nephew; I already knew they were both okay.

—Marjorie, Bolingbrook, Illinois

Mystery of the Roses

There are two events in my life that I consider to be miracles. Both are touched by roses. My mother was widowed young yet raised the four of us with love and faith. Even so, we recognized the special link she had with my older brother, who was also our father's namesake.

Each time one of us added a grandchild to the family, it was an exciting and wonderful time for Mom. But sadly, she suffered a massive stroke at the age of forty-seven and died the same day. On that day also, my older brother's wife learned that she was pregnant with their first child—another grandchild.

When my sister-in-law returned home from the doctor's office that day after getting the good news of her pregnancy, there at the door of their apartment was a single pink rose. No one ever figured out where that rose came from. I like to believe that somehow Mom wanted her son to know she knew. God let it happen.

Roses have also been part of my life, beginning with the rose corsage my husband gave me when we were engaged. But I really understood that years later, when I was in the hospital recovering from surgery. I was feeling down and wishing my husband, Hank, would bring me a rose to show he still loved me.

That evening, when Hank and our daughter visited me, they brought a bouquet from the climbing rosebush in our yard. The miracle wasn't only that Hank brought the flowers. It was that the bush, on the north side of the house and overshadowed by large trees, hadn't blossomed in years. That was in 1979 and the bush hasn't bloomed since. God let that happen, too.

—*Dolores, Roselle, Illinois*

God Who Guides

Thank you, Lord, for the beauty which surrounds us.
Thank you, Lord, that in your beauty, we sometimes seek and
    find direction for our lives.
Open our ears to hear your words of guidance.
Open our eyes to see the signs of your presence around us.
Open our hearts to accept your whispered direction.
The choices life gives us seldom are easy. But grant us the faith
    and the grace to choose wisely,
    listening to you, seeking your guidance.
Amen.

Six

❦

Miracles in the Midst of Disaster

The rains came. And came. And came some more. When they stopped—or rather when they slowed to a merely "normal" storm—the town was awash. TV broadcasters and meteorologists reported that it was a "one-hundred-year storm," a downpour that could be expected only once a century.

Except that our house wasn't there one hundred years ago. Neither were any of the homes on what had been, then, just another piece of anonymous Illinois prairie. Prairie might have been able to handle the water from such a storm. But once that prairie became a neighborhood, the results were disastrous.

There were many stories that April afternoon in 1975. My family's is one of them.

The severity of the storm caught us with little warning. We never would have anticipated that a broad and deep crest of rushing flood-waters would gather at the entrance to the neighborhood, swell with power, and rumble through, seeking its own level—the DuPage River a half mile or so away.

Except that our house was in the way, at the lowest point in the water's path. It happened quickly. The rising tide swept past our split-level house, crashed through the basement windows and filled it. The basement and family room were underwater in minutes as the water lapped at stairs into the kitchen, level with the ground. My wife, Kathy, and our two children barely escaped being trapped in the lower level. Walls were crushed and doors shattered by the force. Appliances shorted out. Our freezer was caught in the current and thrust against the basement ceiling with enough force to stave in its top and dent the ductwork above. A toilet was ripped from its fittings by the torrent. Years of family memories were blotted out, scattered, or lost. There was no insurance, no savings to cover the many, many thousands of dollars in losses and damages. Our home would be uninhabitable for weeks.

Even today the pictures tell a horrible story. While our house was among the worst, there were scores of others in the same area that were damaged. My family was safe. But our lives were in turmoil. Yet it's often in the midst of such shattered realities that God makes himself apparent.

And there were miracles, even as the tragedy unfolded. One found my wife and children huddled in a miraculous dry spot on the front lawn while hip-deep waters surged around them, until friends could wade in and guide them to safety.

The next day dawned gray and overcast. It was very appropriate for our mood. Kathy and I stood at the front door and looked down into the scene of the disaster in the lower levels. We were unsure where to go, where to turn, who to see. The shock was setting in.

Someone phoned our church. The assistant pastor made a call, and within an hour there were a score or more people lending a hand. We had a place to stay. We had people to help shovel out the three thousand books that were now a huge soggy pile. Rugs were carried out; mud was removed from floors, furniture was cleaned and, where necessary, discarded. The lawn looked like a huge junk sale; the garage was littered with broken trash.

There were more miracles. A neighbor lovingly collected every photo in our soaked albums and slaved to dry off each one individually. Only a single picture was lost. The album containing our wedding photos had been destroyed. But the pictures—and the memories—were rescued.

A mechanical genius showed up on the doorstep, toolbox in hand. We didn't know him well then, but he's become a close friend. He cleaned and repaired the furnace, the washer, dryer, and even the damaged freezer.

We saw God.

Disasters have the ability to bring out the best in people. And to help focus flagging faith in God. There's much more to our story. But the miracle was twofold. There was the rescue we experienced. That will forever be a point from which we mark a new beginning, a new journey. It is an event in which we have come to see the working of God in ways that we never would have imagined. Just like another famous flood, this was a milepost on a journey of faith.

There are people who believe they have most been aware of the presence of God in the middle of a terrible disaster. Those are perhaps the miracle stories we most often hear about: the presence of something divine happening in the midst of a tragedy. These are stories that change people by making them aware that there is something more to their lives than getting up each day, working, and going to bed.

In the case of our flood story, the confirmation happened a year later. The anniversary fell on Easter Sunday. It was a joyous holiday but one that was still marked with the barely healed scars of disaster. On Easter Sunday afternoon, after a cloudless and beautiful day, a storm gathered in the east. It brought fears—as thunderstorms did for years afterward—of a repeat of the flood.

But this time, the storm brought a rainbow that stretched from horizon to horizon. God was sending a message.

> And God said, "This is the sign of the covenant I am making between me and you and every living creature with you, a covenant for all generations to come: I have set my rainbow in the clouds, and it will be the sign of the covenant between me and the earth. Whenever I bring clouds over the earth and the rainbow appears in the clouds, I will remember my covenant between me and you and all living creatures of every kind. Never again will the waters become a flood to destroy all life. Whenever the rainbow appears in the clouds, I will see it and remember the everlasting covenant between God and all living creatures of every kind on the earth." (GEN. 9:12–16)

Whirlwind of Death

I was thirteen when six tornadoes blasted through the west Texas town of Sherwood Shores, a retirement trailer village where my grandparents lived. I was staying with them on that fateful weekend.

One of the twisters roared into their trailer home after midnight. It simply exploded. My grandparents, thrown 150 yards by the vicious storm, were the first of many who died that night. When the storm struck, I was blown 250 yards in a different direction. I lay tumbled in the debris until I was found hours later by a rescue party.

Seriously injured and close to death, I was sent by ambulance to a hospital in Amarillo. Even that was an epic adventure, since the ambulance had a flat tire, delaying my treatment while it was changed. In the meantime, my veins had collapsed, and I arrived at the emergency room covered with a sheet and tagged DOA—dead on arrival.

Thank God for short hospital sheets. A physician walking through the area spotted one vein still throbbing in my leg and immediately ordered a transfusion. This was the first step on a long journey of faith and recovery for me.

Many times over the next two weeks, I would be pronounced dead, only to pop back and give another go at life. Among the many injuries I suffered were a broken back, an arm shattered by nine breaks, and—worst of all—my left leg, which had been mangled so badly that it eventually had to be amputated.

But just living through all that isn't the miracle I want to tell.

I was hurt so badly that the doctors didn't want me to know that Grandmother and Grandfather were dead. They feared the shock would kill me. So they wouldn't let Mom and Dad tell me. They didn't have to, because early in the morning on the day of their funeral, I had a vision.

I saw Jesus standing with my grandparents on either side of him. There was no talking in that vision. But I clearly understood when Jesus pointed to an empty spot on the floor in front of him. That spot was for me, it meant, but not just yet. I also knew that my grandparents were happy and that they were at peace.

I was so convinced of what I saw that I called our pastor to come to the hospital. I told him what I had seen and told him to tear up his funeral sermon, because God would tell him what to say from his heart.

He did. I also told my mother when she stopped at the hospital all dressed up for the funeral. I explained that she shouldn't be sad, because they weren't. Later she told me the funeral sermon was exactly what it should have been—not sad but happy.

My recovery was slow but steady. It amazed the doctors, who even told my folks when I was released from the hospital to come home that they shouldn't get their hopes up for me; I still might not make it. Many say it's a miracle that I'm alive. I rather think there were many small miracles along the way.

Well, I was thirteen when it happened, and more than twenty-five years later I'm still here. I have a great husband and two beautiful children. In all those years, I have never asked, "Why me, Lord? Why did I survive when so many others didn't?"

I know there's a special reason that I'm alive, though I may never know those I have helped with my determination and faith. If I have helped one or a hundred and one, that's okay. I know I have a place waiting for me in heaven. I know because I saw it.

—*Sandi, Amarillo, Texas*

Fire in the Classroom!

The Our Lady of the Angels School fire burned itself into the history of Chicago and the country. And it's a story that changed my life and enriched my faith.

It was December 1, 1958. I was in the fifth grade. Twenty minutes before dismissal, a boy suddenly leaped from his seat screaming that smoke was coming from beneath the classroom door. It was the start of the most terrible time of my life. Before it ended, more than ninety-five children and teachers were killed.

When the smoke flowed into our classroom, we all started crying and panicking. In a very calm voice, our teacher instructed us all to remain at our desks and follow her in prayer. She said that God would save us.

I didn't sit down. As I stood at my desk, I felt as though someone were leading me to the windows. The teacher saw me move toward them but never said a word and continued to pray. Very quickly the thick smoke darkened the classroom. I could hear the prayers of my class-mates become weaker and dwindle until there was silence except for the thumping noise of bodies falling against their desks.

Another girl and I were the only two at the window, screaming for help. Every now and then the smoke would billow over our heads and out the window. Both of us were having great difficulty breathing, and I was even beginning to foam at the mouth from inhaling the heavy smoke. Even though I was only ten, I knew then that I might die and never see my family again.

After what seemed like an eternity, firemen came with ladders that were almost too short for our third-floor windows. Petrified though we were, we clambered out over the boiling-hot radiator and were saved.

Most of my classmates in that room and my teacher died in that inferno. Yet I suffered only a few minor burns and nothing else—a mir-acle, considering the hot smoke from the intense fire.

There are two things that, for me, came out of this terrible, horri-ble tragedy.

First, about a week before the fire, a classmate told me she had a sort of vision. She had walked into the closet to get a sweater and said she saw Jesus standing there with a glow surrounding him. He seemed to be beckoning her. But when she turned and walked toward the vision, it faded away.

She told me never to mention it to anyone, because no one would believe her. I promised I wouldn't say anything. A week later she died in the fire and indeed did go home to God. I believe her vision was more than that; I believe it was real.

I survived the fire at Our Lady of the Angels School when lots of others didn't, but the experience also changed me. Many people have told me over the years how lucky I was to be spared. I never considered it luck but rather a miracle. I truly believe God didn't want me in heaven at that time and led me to that window.

That was a long time ago. Now I'm a married woman with two grown children. Except for a miracle, it might not have turned out that way.

—*Carol, Itasca, Illinois*

Dust Bowl Death—and Life

The devastating dust storms of the 1930s turned much of the Great Plains states from the breadbasket of the nation into a desolate desert. They threatened to make the already severe Great Depression even more severe. As the drought deepened, farm families watched as their lands were turned from waving seas of green into shifting dunes of dust.

It was a terrible time for those who lived through it. At its height, the dust bowl affected fifty million acres. It was centered in Kansas, Oklahoma, and Texas but affected states as far north as the Dakotas. Even worse, the wild winds blew curtains of dust throughout the Midwest, and drifts built up against buildings. No one who saw it ever forgot it. Yet through it all, heart and hope remained fresh. This is one of its stories.

I was in nurses' training at Mercy Hospital in Dubuque, Iowa, during the dust storms. Because it was impossible to keep the dust out— it blew through the smallest cracks, beneath doors, around the window frames—we had not been able to do any surgery for several days. Keeping the hospital clean was a challenge. Even chapel benches had to be dusted before the nurses in their white skirts could sit down.

We had all been praying for days for relief; a little rain would end this bout, help settle the dust, and allow us to continue our work.

The niece of the head of the hospital, who had been waiting to deliver her child, gave birth at the height of the dust storm. The child, sadly, was a "blue baby"—having a congenital heart and blood condition which at that time was not survivable. Death was only a matter of time.

It was my assignment to stay with the tiny, struggling infant, who had been named Mary, but I could do nothing except try to make her comfortable. A few days after her birth, it became evident that little Mary was dying. I stood by the crib with her aunt, whose prayer was simple and heartfelt: "Little Mary, when you get to heaven, ask our Lord to send us some rain." That was all; there was nothing else to say.

A few minutes later as Mary gasped her last breath, her aunt held up her finger for me to listen as raindrops began to splatter on the nursery window. It was the rain that ended the dry spell. The dust storms abated and the grass grew again.

—Jeanette, Mendota, Illinois

Derailment, Death, and Discovery

NEWS ITEM: Amtrak's Sunset Limited, a sleek, eleven-car red-and-silver passenger train traveling between Los Angeles and Miami, barreled off a bridge in Alabama before dawn on September 22, 1993. The bridge, damaged when a barge struck it in the darkness only minutes before, collapsed when the train sped onto the span. The train's three engines and four of the passenger cars plunged into the water and mud of Big Bayou, killing 47 people and injuring 103 others.

I was asleep when the Amtrak train derailed around three a.m. that fateful morning. It was a terrifying moment for everyone on board. It felt as though we had boarded a roller coaster or were going over bumps on the highway at high speed. Suddenly there was a bright flash of light and a metal-on-metal grinding, as though the train were trying to drag itself to a stop.

Then I felt the car shudder and we began to slide off the rails sideways. Water splashed into the car and filled it up to our waists. I figured we had fallen into a river somewhere. A woman's voice cried out in the pitch-black darkness, "Oh God, we're all going to die!"

I was on a trip that had been put off for years. My late sister's family had repeatedly asked me to visit, but I hadn't seen them for five years, ever since my sister's death. I have always considered train travel to be relaxing and interesting, so I finally made reservations on the Sunset Limited. I boarded the train in San Antonio and was scheduled to arrive in Jacksonville to see my nephew the next afternoon.

God had other plans.

After we landed in the river, everything seemed to stop. We didn't know it at the time, but the car we were in was being held out of the water by only a huge wooden beam from the bridge. A couple of men found a flashlight and moved to an emergency exit window, which they removed so we could clamber out.

A young man named Michael went through the window, sat on the ledge astride it, and asked me, "Can you swim?" I said I couldn't. He explained that I would have to jump from the window and that although I would go under the water, he would hold on to my arm. I trusted him and jumped. He did hold on, and when we came to the surface, he swam with me to a piece of debris about thirty feet away. Others from the car were already there, holding on or sitting on it, trying to understand what had happened.

We quickly saw that the car directly in front of ours was engulfed in flames fed by the diesel fuel tanks in the locomotives. Bits and pieces of burned debris floated all around us. We wondered whether the diesel fuel would drift our way and burn away our little island of safety. All I could think about was the TV show *Rescue 911.*

A tugboat located our refuge and brought us to safety. The scary part was over, though we still had the ordeal of being brought back to civilization, checked out at the hospital, clothed, fed, and cared for before being sent on our way. There was still the media and the TV reporters to contend with. I never knew until I arrived home how many people in San Antonio were watching. My life has not been the same since; I am frequently pointed out as "that woman who survived the Amtrak accident."

Yet the crash was an experience that has given me plenty of food for thought, some of which I want to share with others.

Why wasn't I one of the forty-seven who died? That continues to haunt me.

How did that piece of timber come to be wedged into the car I was in, to keep it upright and above water? How was it that Andrea, an eleven-year-old girl with cerebral palsy, landed safely in the coach stairwell from the bottom floor? How could I have remained so calm throughout the ordeal once the train came to a halt? It's beyond my comprehension.

The experience of having so many people tell me they prayed, wept, and rejoiced for me has been very moving. The countless hugs and kisses and teary-eyed people have had me all but breathless and in awe. I am still overwhelmed by it. I continue to wonder and ponder, *What is this that God is allowing to happen to me?*

Yet I hope to continue to reflect more clearly on my "new" life— or as some say, my new "baptism." When I saw the request for people to share their small miracles, I wanted to share this one.

Nor is my experience over. Since the Amtrak adventure, I am discovering many Scripture verses that have a new and different meaning for me and that suddenly grab my attention. For instance, reading the gospel account of Jesus stopping the storm and of the calm that followed is especially significant.

—*Sister Adele, San Antonio, Texas*

Without warning, a furious storm came up on the lake, so that the waves swept over the boat. But Jesus was sleeping. The disciples went and woke him, saying, "Lord, save us! We're going to drown!"

He replied, "You of little faith, why are you so afraid?" Then he got up and rebuked the winds and the waves, and it was completely calm. (MATT. 8:24–26)

Lord of the Storm

You calm the furies which rush about us, Lord;
    you smooth our way, even against the winds of life.
When all about us is shattered and torn,
    we can turn to you, a rock of safety, a port in the storm.
Lord, thank you for your protection, your refuge, your salvation.
In our tragedies, we turn to you —
    and are comforted.
Amen.

Seven

❧

Miracles of Answered Prayer

*F*ish stories are a great American art form. There are even fish stories—and to some, fishy stories—in Scripture. Most such tales, both in Scripture and in life, are full of emotion, excuses, and excitement. Not all, however, suffer from the fisherman's sense of exaggeration. This is one of those.

It happened in San Francisco Bay, a long way from the Sea of Galilee, the site of quite another fish story. This story only works because Bob and his friend John (whom they call "the Baptist," because he is) are fishermen with big mouths. Bob, who lives in Oakland, California, told me it happened like this:

Bob and John volunteered to help out in a local ecumenical soup kitchen. It was work they enjoyed, because of the interaction they got to have with the residents. One day, they described one of their favorite recipes to some of the homeless people; it was a mouthwatering Cajun fish stew. Everyone seemed interested, so they promised to fix it for the two hundred people who eat there.

That was almost a mistake.

Let's see: two hundred people at a quarter pound each equals fifty pounds of fish, raw, fresh from the water. At least, according to the recipe. When they promised to make the meal for the residents of the shelter, they figured on using a local favorite, striped bass. They could catch them in the bay a lot cheaper than it would cost to buy the fish. Except striped bass only average about nine pounds each and have a two-fish-per-day-per-fisherman legal limit. Besides, it was late August and the fishing was very slow.

A problem.

That's the same boat—you should pardon the pun—another big-mouthed fisherman, the apostle Peter, once found himself in. He'd just come back from a fishing trip with no fish. That's already enough to put anyone in a bad mood. After all, for him fishing wasn't a hobby; it was a livelihood. But as he came back empty-handed—or empty-boated— HE DISCOVERED THIS GUY ON THE BEACH WITH A WHOLE LOT OF PEOPLE FOLLOWING HIM.

Without so much as an invitation, the man gets into the boat and tells Peter to push off a little way so he can continue talking to the crowds. Maybe the most surprising part of this story is that Peter didn't toss his uninvited guest into the drink. Instead, he went along with the game.

After the fellow is finished talking, he tells Peter, "Throw your nets over thataway. You'll get a big catch." Yeah, right. It's not hard to imagine the response from Peter, a veteran fisherman. And Peter, rough man of the water, was undoubtedly less polite than Saint Luke tells it. But it went something like this: "What? You outta your head? I make my life doing this, and I couldn't bring in so much as a minnow. Besides, what do you know about fishing? You're a carpenter."

There is where our two fish stories come together. Human nature is a wonderful thing. It's amazing the chances we'll take, the risks we'll endure, to avoid embarrassment or to look as if we know what we're doing when we don't. Even better if we can blame someone else for our failures.

If you listen, you can almost hear Peter's words echoing across that big lake—because we've all heard them, and many of us have spoken them: "Okay, I'll do it. But if it doesn't work, you're the one who's gonna look like a fool, not me."

Human nature sometimes requires an extra oomph, a kick in the pants, to encourage us to do what we're supposed to do. For Bob and John, it was the embarrassment of not living up to their boasts.

Embarrassment and shame are great motivations. But they're negatives. The gospel is a positive. So are stories of small miracles. What might begin with the human failings of embarrassment and shame can be transformed positively, with the spirit of faith, into challenge and empowerment.

Hey, it worked for Peter. He caught lots of fish.

> When he had finished speaking, he said to Simon [Peter], "Put out into deep water, and let down the nets for a catch."
>
> Simon answered, "Master, we've worked hard all night and haven't caught anything. But because you say so, I will let down the nets."
>
> When they [Simon and his crew] had done so, they caught such a large number of fish that their nets began to break. So they signaled their partners in the other boat to come and help them, and they came and filled both boats so full that they began to sink.
>
> When Simon Peter saw this, he fell at Jesus' knees and said, "Go away from me, Lord; I am a sinful man!" For he and all his

companions were astonished at the catch of fish they had taken, and so were James and John, the sons of Zebedee, Simon's partners.

Then Jesus said to Simon, "Don't be afraid; from now on you will catch men." (LUKE 5:4–10)

And it worked for Bob and John in California. They'd made that promise to the people at the soup kitchen, and they had to keep it. Because if they didn't … well, they didn't want to even think about facing the folks at the homeless shelter. So here's what took place:

On the day they'd set to go fishing, Bob couldn't go, leaving the task to John alone. Remember, stripers average nine pounds each, limit of two, and he needed fifty pounds. The math simply doesn't work. Besides, the fishing was lousy. None of the other boats out on the bay were bringing in anything, either. So John went where no one else was. He made two casts. The first brought in a thirty-eight-pounder. The second hooked a twelve-pounder.

Now, that math works.

I guess we could say it also worked for those two hundred homeless men, women, and children, who feasted on delicious Cajun fish stew, because they saw and tasted how God honors promises.

Prayer is often how we beseech miracles. People pray differently. Some pray quietly, expectantly. Others use well-worn words and phrases from childhood. Still others pray with their hands as they work for some goal. Sometimes, like Bob and John, we find ourselves in uncomfortable situations. We might face embarrassment. Or, as in some of the miracle stories that follow, life itself might be out of control, heading down the wrong path.

Changed Hearts, Changed Lives

For years I worked in the front office of our small school here in upstate New York. I was receptionist, attendance officer, computer user, and telephone operator. I was the first person people saw when they came through the door. And I loved my job.

In the next office was the principal's secretary. We—and I mean this quite literally—hated each other. Our hatred was like a festering sore, and it had gone on for four long years. Don't think I'm exaggerating; I'm not.

The hate I felt for her kept me from being peaceful. I'd go home at night and think up ways to "get even." This wasn't just me, either; it was mutual. How I despised her; she tried to prove I was inadequate, and I tried to prove she was incompetent. Our glares and leers kept up every minute of every day. Our boss, the school principal, threatened to fire us both if we didn't stop feuding.

I didn't want to be like this. I'm really not a bad person. But I became afraid that the Devil really had hold of me. I tried—and failed—to fight this scourge by myself. One day on my way back to work from an errand, I decided to try something new—prayer. The conversation went like this, word for word (because I remember every bit of it, even today):

"I need help. I can't live with this hatred inside of me. I can't shake it away. I'm not vicious. But I can't do it alone. I'm not strong enough; only you can help me. I don't want to die with this hatred. I want peace. Please. I'm scared."

I began sobbing and cried all the way back to work that day, pleading in prayer for a miracle.

When I arrived in school, I went straight to my nemesis' office and said, "Hi." She said, "Good morning." There was no mean feeling. I looked right at her and honestly felt no animosity. It was like being cured of cancer.

I had been relieved of this ugly hate. I was calm, happy. She could tell I had changed. And you know, she changed, too. Now we're friends. We often share lunch and joke about how we hated each other. I tell everyone who notices the difference that it was prayer that changed me. People in school say, "I see you two are speaking now." I answer, "You won't understand, but it's a miracle."

—*Catherine, Huletts Landing, New York*

Running on Empty

I'd been caring for my aged mother for several years. She suffered from Alzheimer's disease, and as her conditioned worsened, she became more and more susceptible to pneumonia. As a result, we had to be very careful in the cold weather, something we get lots of here around Saratoga, New York.

When the winter was at its worst, our tank of heating oil was down to a quarter full. We knew from experience that this meant it would only last about four more cold days. We had no money; my salesman husband hadn't sold anything. Dreading the journey every day, I went downstairs to check the level. And every day it still registered a quarter full.

I kept this up for two weeks, praying each time, and the meter never left the quarter-full mark. Finally my husband made a sale, got some money, and we called for an oil delivery. Just as the tanker drove up to begin filling the tank, I checked the level. Empty. But in minutes the tank was full again, and the house was nice and warm for Mom.

I didn't tell many people about this. They probably would have thought I was nuts. However, miracles do happen; all we need is a little faith.

—*Mary, Ballston Spa, New York*

Love Lost, Love Found

I've never seen the sun dance, like a few people say they have. And I've never been cured from a deadly disease, like others claim. But I've seen a miracle just the same.

My adventure began in the late 1980s when I was a sophomore in college. I had been in love, but we broke up. It was very painful. To distract myself from the agony of losing him, I went on a diet. I lost weight—lots of it—but also developed an eating disorder. I didn't mean for that to happen; no one ever does. I got into treatment, which seemed to be working. I even made friends with another girl in the group.

All my friendships had pretty much dissolved because of my eating problems. I believed people were talking behind my back and that my friends thought I was crazy because I was getting counseling. I distrusted everyone at school and eventually moved out of the dorm to rent an apartment with my new friend, Carol.

This was a turning point in my life. But it was a turn for the worse.

I started smoking, drinking, and sleeping around. Though we were only nineteen, Carol and I had no trouble getting into bars. And that became our routine every weekend.

You need to understand how unlike me this was. I never drank in high school and was very close to God. I had planned to remain a virgin until I married. But when I lost that first love, it threw me for such a loop that my life went spinning out of control.

Throughout my junior year in college, our weekends started on Thursday night and were a blur of drinking and sex. Even though I began to realize what was happening and that my life wasn't right, I couldn't do anything. I couldn't go back to church, because I believed I was too much of a sinner. Carol and I had become so dependent on each other that it was unhealthy. It got to the point where I couldn't go out and not get very drunk.

I know God tried to show himself to me during those terrible months. But I also know I couldn't respond. Then one Sunday morning I awoke after a particularly tawdry Saturday night and decided I was going to go to church. It was as if I were going for the first time. Everything was so beautiful that I cried and prayed through most of it.

That same day, a really nice guy from one of my classes invited me swimming. His name was Bob, and that turned out to be only our first date. Others followed. Bob didn't drink at all, so when we were together, I didn't have to deal with alcohol. I felt like my old self again. The only good thing about my life was my relationship with Bob, and I was terrified I would do something to mess it up.

Carol didn't like the change in me at all. Even though I went with Bob other nights, she insisted that we still make the rounds of the bars on Friday nights. Saturday through Thursday I would do well, but every Friday night I would go out with Carol and get drunk. I'd go out and couldn't stop myself. I was caught in a cycle I couldn't escape.

I wasn't going to church very much during this terrible time. But I would often pray the Lord's Prayer. When I got to the end, where it says, "deliver us from evil," I would always add, "deliver *me* from *this* evil." I felt trapped. I knew I loved Bob, and he was the man I wanted to spend my life with. But every Friday, without fail, I would go out with Carol and get drunk.

After more than two years of being messed up, I discovered I was pregnant. Bob and I were going to have a baby. Bob quickly asked me to marry him. "Of course," I said. "Yes!!" Overnight I stopped drinking and smoking and started going back to church. In the year that followed, I got married, graduated from college, and had my first child.

I was very scared at the time, but as I look back, I can see the hand of God so clearly. I found a path out of the terrible cycle of self-destruction. Our daughter is beautiful and is a joy and a blessing. When I think about how I prayed, asking God to deliver me from evil, and how he did it so completely, I am filled with awe and gratitude. This has been the greatest miracle of my life. Bob is wonderful and we have had a second child, a son. We have become strong in our faith and close to God.

I want everyone to know of God's mercy and that no one is too big a sinner to go to him.

—*M., Des Moines, Iowa*

with her group. It was an outing that scared me, but I decided to go, believing I was in God's hands.

One afternoon, a friend and I were sitting on the deck listening to a group of Irish entertainers. Suddenly a squall came up. Wind and rain pelted the ship. Within moments, people scattered and the deck cleared. My friend said, "Let's hurry and get inside."

I replied, almost without thinking, "No. We'll be fine." So we stayed and continued chatting, oblivious to the wind and rain and darkness.

It wasn't long before the sun broke through and people started coming back outside. They saw us and exclaimed, "Look! Look at this circle." For the first time, I noticed that my friend and I sat within a circle of dryness surrounded by puddles. I was not surprised, because I have come to believe that God is with me. I was safe and never doubted him.

—*Mary, Levittown, New York*

Getting Her Life on Track

My children were small when we had to leave my husband because he had started taking heavy drugs. Two tries at rehabilitation didn't cure him.

I knew I had to look to the future and enrolled in college to work toward my degree. I would be able to get financial aid for the following semester, but getting through the first one would be tough. I was already in debt and didn't want to borrow more. I prayed, but instead of an answer, I simply felt comfortable with the situation; it would work out. I sensed that I was not to put limits on how God would make everything all right, just trust that it would be okay.

Toward the end of the semester, my sister invited me to her home. Driving there, I passed a racehorse track and felt a sudden and strange urge to go there instead. This was foreign to me; I am not a bettor and I don't gamble. I checked my wallet and the gas gauge. I had enough gas and a ten-dollar bill. I went to the track. I'd never been there before.

Parking the car, I wondered how much admission was and how much of my ten dollars it would cost. But it was late and no one was collecting. As I walked in, the numbers four and seven jumped into my mind. The fifth race was over, so I guessed that I should put my ten dollars on the fourth horse in the seventh race.

I did. The horse won and paid forty to one. I walked away with $440. My tuition was $390 and I needed $50 to buy books for the next semester.

That happened a long time ago. My children are grown and I've completed more education, earning a master's degree. But I still remember standing there quaking as the horse trotted around the track, afraid that God was going to get me that tuition money—and equally afraid that he wouldn't. It amazed me that prayer can be so easy. You simply pray and leave it to God to bring it about. It seems to help not trying to tell God how he should help. Many people think gambling is evil and wouldn't have responded to those urgings as I did. And for them that may be right. But this miracle provided money when I needed it and guidance that I was on the right track. No pun intended—at least, not by me.

—*J. C., Nassau, New York*

First Snow of Winter

Even for people who live in areas that see lots of snow, the first storm of the season is always the hardest to get used to. It seems as if we need a refresher course in winter driving skills. One day, after a visit to my aunt's home ten miles away from mine, my two young daughters and I were not happy to be returning home in the first snow of the winter. The road has a very steep and winding stretch that passes our church and the school my daughters attended.

As we approached the hill, we could see many cars stuck on the way up and others spinning as they tried to come down. The girls were scared and wanted to know why I was maneuvering around stalled and stopped cars. Like them, I was frightened. I told them that if I stopped, we would be stuck like all the rest. To calm them, I suggested they pray that we would get home safely.

The oldest girl, Vickie, was in the front seat with me. She ducked beneath the dashboard and prayed quietly. Valerie stood up in the backseat behind me, her hands clutched almost too tightly around my throat, shouting the Lord's Prayer into my ear. We had begun to lose speed approaching the crest, and I was afraid we too would become victims of the hill and the snow, which was blinding now and beginning to drift and fill in the side of the road. Suddenly I had an idea. As we slid toward the curb, I would bounce the car off it. That would give us enough additional momentum to get us over the top. Sure enough, it worked; we reached flat roadway and safety.

The following week we again were driving home from another visit. There was no snow this time and the driving was a snap. As we got to the hilly spot where we could see our church, I announced, "Look everyone, here's where we bounced the car off the curb to make it over the hill."

But to our amazement, there was no curb on the street.

—*Joanne, Girard, Ohio*

Blue Jean Blues

School was beginning, the weather was getting cooler, and my son had outgrown all his jeans over the summer. At any other time, a quick trip to the store would have solved the problem, but my husband had been unemployed for more than a year, and even a pair of jeans would have strained the slim family budget.

Before shopping, I said a quick prayer for help to find cheap but good jeans. The mall had advertised some, but even the sale price was beyond my means. I suddenly had an inspiring thought: resale shop. I walked in with confidence—surely this was an answer to my prayer. But I walked out without jeans. Oh, they had stacks, but none in the right size.

There is a Bible promise that if we give with charity, we will be blessed to overflowing. Remembering how generously I had given to clothing collections at church when we had more, I was hoping that now, when I needed it most, I would find that blessing.

The next day, I decided to try other resale shops in our area. As I prepared to leave the house, a friend rang the doorbell, holding three pairs of blue jeans. "Luke outgrew these," she said. "And I thought they might fit Jonathan." They did.

Some small miracles need people open to God's whisper for assistance, to help them happen.

—*Judy, Mount Prospect, Illinois*

Out of Harm's Way

I just had to tell the story of my miracle. It happened during the 1970s when my husband and I lived near an air force bombing range in south central Florida. I was in my twenties and had grown away from my church and regular prayer.

One Saturday afternoon, I had agreed to take several of the neighborhood kids on a bicycle ride to the bombing range. It was a lovely but isolated stretch of country. We had ridden about five miles out when we decided to return home.

Turning the bikes around, we were horrified to see a huge thunderhead bearing down on us. Anyone who has lived in southern Florida—sometimes called the lightning capital of the world—knows how quickly and how powerfully such storms are born.

I didn't know what to do. I had several smaller children with me, and I felt responsible for their safety. They were tiring quickly, and I knew we couldn't beat the storm back to shelter. We could huddle together by the side of the road, but that would offer scant protection from the lightning strikes that typically occur during these severe summer storms.

I just prayed for help to guide these children to safety, because I knew I couldn't do it myself. God's answer came quickly, even more quickly than the storm. Around the bend drove an unscheduled security patrol that "just happened by," as the driver explained. All the kids, bikes, and I fit snugly in the back of the pickup. We were home by the time the rain began to fall.

—*Elizabeth, Post Falls, Idaho*

A Musical Miracle

There have been lots of little miracles in my life so far and lots of interesting "coincidences." But a special one popped into my mind. A few years ago I was unable to come up with the $235 monthly rent for the one-room apartment I was living in. Relatives offered me a sleeping room in their home until I could get on my feet. The understanding was that it might take as long as a year. I didn't make much money but had agreed to pay them the same amount—$235 a month—that I had been paying. Of course, if I was a little late, I wouldn't be put out on the street.

I didn't have much in the way of "stuff"—furniture and household goods. Still, it was too much for the small sleeping room. I wanted to hang on to my chair and table and kitchen things, so I stored them in my brother's basement, several miles away.

I began saving for a deposit on an apartment. But it was hard to gather that much money, and as the months passed, my relatives were getting impatient—and rightly so.

I found a nice little place that "just happened" to be available, and the landlord only wanted a month's rent—and no deposit would be needed. I could handle that, so I collected all my belongings from my brother and moved into my new place.

I unpacked one of the boxes that had some vases, religious articles, and books. But it was late and I decided to call it a day. I put everything back into the box except for one little statue. There's nothing particularly remarkable about that statue; it is a music box with Mary holding the Christ child.

Please understand that the statue is not battery operated; it's spring driven. You wind it up and it plays. It had been stored more than two years. And—I tested this later—because it's driven by a windup spring, it rarely starts or stops at the beginning of a refrain.

I was sitting in my very old—but my very own—armchair. The apartment was quiet and it was mine. I didn't have a TV and the radio was off. And I was a bit overwhelmed, frightened, and wondering if I could make it here.

At that very moment, with no one touching it, the music box played its comforting hymn—from beginning to end. It felt good.

I've been here now for six months. The rent has always been paid on time, and everything is getting better, little by little.

—*Ed, Altona, Indiana*

The Dream

My sister Joan was born with Down's syndrome. She was a sickly child, and doctors told my parents she would not live beyond seven years old. They were wrong; she died a few years ago, just shy of her sixtieth birthday.

It was the love of family and friends and the constant care she received from my Mom that allowed her to live a full and happy life.

After the deaths of our parents, Joan made her home with my husband and me for eight years. She became very ill and had to be confined in a nursing home until she died peacefully while I held her hand.

On the night she died I had a dream. I was back in our hometown. I was crossing a street, with Joan holding on to my hand. I saw my mother walking toward us. Then I realized Joan had let go of my hand. I started to panic, fearing I had lost her. But then, in the dream, my mother assured me that I hadn't lost her at all.

I watched as my mother and my sister walked slowly away from me. I know this was God's way of letting me know that the two truly were together. I'll never forget the dream. I didn't confide in many people, but I firmly believe it was a small miracle, and it left me with a sense of peace and serenity. Joan was safely home.

—*Marie, Mendham, New Jersey*

Lord Who Listens

Your word to us is consistent and clear—
> "Ask and it will be given to you; seek and you will find;
> knock and the door will be opened to you" (Matt. 7:7).
Why, Lord, are we sometimes so afraid to
> ask, to seek?
Is it because if we ask and do not hear,
> or seek and still lose our way, that part of our being may
doubt you?

How foolish of us. How distrustful of your abounding love.
Help us, Lord, to trust in your listening presence.
Give us open ears and a listening heart to heed your answers.
Amen.

Eight

❦

Miracles of the Angels

Darkness is the emptiest, most crowded place in human existence. A contradiction? Hardly. I've been there. I suspect most of us have.

My own experience with oppressive, empty, yet crowded darkness came one night in the army. I stood guard duty on a moonless, overcast, lightless night. We were simulating combat conditions; we could use no light. The darkness was so palpable that I could feel my eyes wandering in my head, unable to focus. I could see neither ground nor sky, neither horizon nor even my rifle in front of me. Had I not been holding it, I would have surely lost it.

I was alone, even though surrounded by hundreds of my comrades-in-arms.

Yet, being alone, I felt pressed in on all sides by some giant, all-encompassing crowd. It was terrible. And it was fascinating. I couldn't properly fulfill my official guard duties—I could see nothing, and my other senses were so fogged by the overpowering sense of darkness that I doubt I could have heard anything. As I wavered in an abyss, somewhere between fear and panic, suddenly there was a flicker of brightness, a match light across the camp, hundreds of yards away.

A cook preparing for breakfast had lit a cigarette. He was breaking the rules, but finally I was able to focus on something. It returned my senses of up, down, here and there. That light placed me again in the universe; I knew where I was. And I was able to keep my place until the dark was itself chipped away, overpowered slowly by the inexorable approach of dawn.

I was young and didn't realize the depth of the experience until years later. I didn't understand that it was a replay of all the fears and battles humankind has had with the darkness, both physical and spiritual.

Darkness has always been an enemy. We have long fought it, sought to banish it. There's no wonder that battle has occupied a large part of our religious tradition. We have made light the sign of good, and darkness the sign of all that isn't good. Our God is a God of light. The scriptural imagery is pervasive.

> The Spirit of the Sovereign LORD is on me,
> because the LORD has anointed me
> to preach good news to the poor.
> He has sent me to bind up the brokenhearted,
> to proclaim freedom for the captives
> and release from darkness for the prisoners.
>
> —ISA. 61:1

> When Jesus spoke again to the people, he said, "I am the light of the world. Whoever follows me will never walk in darkness, but will have the light of life." (JOHN 8:12)

We have come to understand that, in our faith-history and our present understanding, messengers of the light are called angels. But when the darkness closes in, we often begin to grasp at flickers of light. Just ask Catherine, a college student from McAllen, Texas. She understands.

"Texas nights in the back country without a moon are the darkest in the world," she told me. "It was on a night like that, dark and foreboding and empty, that I heard an angel's voice. I know we Texans can stretch a yarn, but most of what we say is true. I know this is."

This is her story.

Catherine explained that the road between her home in McAllen and Pan American College (Edinburg, Texas), where she attended classes, was a beautiful country drive in the daytime. But that particular night, it was unusually dark. Her car's headlights didn't even seem to penetrate it.

"Suddenly a feeling of immediate terror and danger swept over me. I recognized it. Once before, I'd had the same sense while driving and had slammed on the brakes, barely in time to avoid an accident. Because I knew better than to shrug off that strange sensation, I reacted the same way: I jammed my foot onto the brake pedal, and my car slithered to a stop," she said.

That's when she looked up and saw the repeated flashes of freight cars speeding by, mere feet in front of her car. "As I sat in the dark listening to the rhythmic clickity-clack of the steel wheels on the rails, I felt flushed and wrung out. I knew I had come closer to danger than ever before. Or since, for that matter," Catherine said.

"Many people would call this strong feeling an intuition. But I want to give credit where credit is due. I believe an angel of God was watching over me. I can never tell this story often enough. It's how I say thanks."

Darkness happens to us all. Those who have faith will sometimes find themselves led out of that darkness. And for some, it is an angel who does the leading. Angels—as messengers of God—are an important tradition in many faiths. They are present in the stories of the Bible, in both the Old and New Testaments. In most cases, they are simply visitors who do good.

In some Christian traditions, each believer is "assigned" a guardian angel to protect that person from harm, a sort of conscience with wings. But as these stories indicate, the angels may be closer than we think. What we perceive to be angelic intervention usually happens in crisis, like a bolt of light piercing the darkness. That is, I suppose, appropriate for a being of light, a messenger of the God of light.

Angel or Samaritan?

If I dwell more on fact than emotions in my story, you'll have to excuse me. I'm a financial analyst, and that sort of thing comes naturally.

The story I'm about to tell does not have a happy beginning. Both of my parents were in the same hospital, on different floors. The horror of watching Dad on a ventilator, fighting for every breath, and seeing Mom die little by little of cancer each day cannot be described. My sister, brother, and I were on scheduled shifts for both parents, since we felt it important that one of us be with each of them. With jobs and personal commitments, it was not easy. It pushed us to the limits of our faith and endurance, but we did it.

The day of the angel was such a day—long, full, exhausting.

It had begun when I relieved my sister at four a.m. I stayed with Mom until nine that morning, worked a full day, and returned to Dad's bedside at six-thirty in the evening. At nine I relieved my brother in Mom's room and stayed until my sister returned at eleven-thirty. All I could think about was going home and to bed.

The hospital's elevators were notoriously slow. That night as I waited for one to arrive, I noticed a man standing behind me. The elevator came and the two of us joined a tall man who was already in the car. Both seemed to be watching me, and I felt very conscious of my dress and high heels. What a terrible disadvantage. I always feel weak in a dress and heels and strong in jeans and tennis shoes, but I'd had no time to change.

I was wary of both, and when the elevator reached the first floor, I held back so they would leave ahead of me. It didn't work, and as we left the hospital for the parking lot, they were both still behind me. I had the strong feeling I was about to face a dangerous situation and felt my senses sharpen, and I became increasingly tense.

It was well-lit near the hospital, but I had parked on the side of the parking lot where it was quite deserted. I breathed a quick prayer as I set out, since I was certain both men were shadowing me. Once again I wished for sweats and tennis shoes.

Halfway down the lot toward my car, I was approached by a middle-aged woman who came right up to me and said, "Can you help me, please? I'm driving my daughter's car and don't know how to turn on the lights." I am generally suspicious of anyone approaching me in that manner, no matter how harmless they may seem, but she appeared genuinely distressed and reminded me of my Mom. I went over to her car, leaned in, and switched on the lights for her. It was simple, since I had once owned a similar vehicle.

I thought the two men had passed me. Then I looked around for the woman, but her car was gone. Instead, I saw that both my shadows were right behind me. The man who had waited for the elevator with me began a conversation by asking if I had a family member on the floor we had both visited. I said that, yes, my mother was a patient.

By now, the other man had reached us and passed by, giving the man I was with a terribly sour look. My new companion watched the other man sweep past, turned back to me, and said, "You shouldn't be walking to your car unescorted late at night," and he urged me to get security to go with me in the future. "With all that's going on in your life now, you don't need a personal tragedy," he said.

I thanked him, got into my car, and drove away.

But this adventure wasn't over.

I was reflecting about how this Good Samaritan appeared out of nowhere to save me from a potentially dangerous situation, when my car suddenly died a few blocks from the hospital. The car wouldn't even coast. Once again conscious of how I was dressed, I got out, locked the car, and began to walk back to the hospital, which was still in sight.

Almost immediately I spotted a group of youths who, by their hoots and yells, obviously saw me, too. They turned and began coming my way. Just as I was about to kick off those blasted high heels and flee barefoot for my life, a car pulled up. It was my Good Samaritan, who calmly said, "Need help?"

We drove back to my disabled car. He suggested we push it into the lot of a nearby hotel, where it would be out of the way. He said the manager was a friend of his and that the car could remain overnight. In the hotel, he talked to a tall, thin, black-haired young man, who handed me a parking ticket stub and let me use the phone to call my husband.

I thanked my rescuer once again and told him that he'd certainly been my guardian angel that night. I still remember the smile and the look he gave me when I said that. He left and I waited for my husband. Later when I couldn't sleep because of the excitement, I remembered I had never even asked his name.

I was determined to find out who my guardian angel was, so the next day I went back to the hotel and spoke to the manager. I explained what had happened and that the night manager had arranged for my car to be left overnight. I figured he could tell me who the man was so I could thank him more formally.

But the manager knew nothing about the incident and didn't know who had given me the parking stub and let me use the phone. In fact, the night manager on duty that evening was a red-haired woman. Yes, it was their parking ticket, but no one resembling the tall, thin, black-haired man I described worked there.

I have turned the events of this night over and over in my mind. Some things clicked and some didn't. In reading about other people's experiences with guardian angels, a common thread seemed to be that a person who has been aided by such an angel first has had the opportunity to help someone else. I thought of the woman who asked me to help with her car lights. It was such a small thing to do, but I was so leery. I remember how quickly she disappeared, and I didn't see her pass me.

Between the time my protector rescued me in the parking lot and when he showed up by my disabled car was at least five minutes. By all rights, he should have been long gone from the area. And of course, who was it at the hotel who helped me? Not an employee, obviously.

Good Samaritan or guardian angel? I can only say that he was a help to me during one of the lowest points of my life. The realization that I was living under God's care was like a shot in the arm. My faith, which had been at the breaking point as I watched my parents' suffering, was strengthened. My soul, which was at risk of becoming hard and bitter, became instead soft and yielding. God's healing power was not for my parents; rather, it was for my spirit and enabled me to face their deaths with my faith intact.

—*Anita, Des Moines, Iowa*

Trust in the Lord

I will never forget the greatest challenge to my faith. Our fourteen-year-old daughter became ill with what seemed to be just a severe case of the flu. But when I brought her to our local emergency room, the attending doctor told us it was Reye's Syndrome, a serious complication. I immediately understood that we could lose her.

The next few hours passed in a dizzying blur of trying to locate my out-of-town husband, consulting with specialists, signing releases for treatment including a brain shunt and life support. Doctors transferred her to another hospital, which had experience treating Reye's Syndrome. As I watched the ambulance pull away, I felt distraught and alone.

My husband and I spent the next few days at the bedside of our beautiful daughter, a respirator breathing for her, and a bank of monitors checking her cranial pressure and other life signs. If she survived—still a big question—there could be severe brain damage.

Only occasionally did we leave the pediatric intensive care ward to visit the chapel or sit in a nearby lounge with our family, friends, and clergy, who came to offer us support and prayer. After one such visit, I was alone in a hospital corridor, when seemingly out of nowhere, a smiling black man approached me.

He immediately began to talk, telling me how he had come to the hospital to volunteer. I was preoccupied with returning to my daughter's side and was only half listening, when I was gripped by what he said next: "Everything's going to be all right. You have to trust in the Lord."

And then he was gone.

I was stunned as I realized I had not said a word; there was no way he could have known what my situation was.

I returned in a daze to my husband and recounted the incident. I remember saying to him as I finished the story, "That was God." Afterwards we were really able to trust that the Lord would take care of our daughter. We didn't know how, or what, would happen—or when. But we knew it would be okay. We just knew.

We were at her side when she awoke from the coma. She survived with no ill effects at all, and we will forever be thankful.

But not a day goes by that I don't think of the jovial man who brought me the message to trust in the Lord. I will never know if he was an angel, but I am humbled to realize I was gifted by this direct contact with the hand of God.

Thank you for the opportunity to share my miracle with others. I hope it will open the eyes of those who are having difficulty "seeing" that God is active in their lives.

—*Cathy, Watseka, Illinois*

On the Arm of an Angel

The story of my angel began eighteen years ago. I was nursing my bedridden mother three days before Christmas and asked her what she wanted as a present on that day. She replied that she wanted a picture of Jesus holding a lamb.

Thankfully, the image was not a hard one to find. That's not the miracle. After having the picture wrapped, I headed home, happy I would be able to give Mom something she wanted.

At a busy boulevard on the way, I stopped, pressed the pedestrian-walk button, and stepped off the curb when the "Go" sign came on. Suddenly a car came racing down the hill, heedless of the traffic signal. I knew there was no one else around, so you can imagine my surprise when a strong hand yanked me back to the sidewalk and out of harm's way.

The man who was attached to the hand steadied me on my wobbly feet and helped me across the street to my bus stop. Seeing how shaky

I still was, he offered to buy me a cup of coffee at the corner lunch counter until I felt well enough to go on.

I asked his name. He only smiled and said, "Call me your guardian angel." He left me at the counter, saying, "God bless you and your ill mother," and disappeared. I think now I'm a real believer. You see, I never told him my mother was sick. Thank you for letting me relive this awesome experience; it has stayed with me all these years.

—*Judy, Oakland, California*

A Voice in the Dark

About thirty-five years ago, never before and never since, I experienced a miracle. Reflecting on it as I have done many times in the intervening years, I've become certain it was my guardian angel. I don't know what else it could have been.

I was driving home late at night, tired after a full day's work. I confess that I exceeded the speed limit, but there were seldom any cars on the road that late. I had returned to work soon after the birth of my son, because my newly graduated husband had not yet found a job with his economics degree.

I was coming to a place where I would turn off the highway. It's not a normal corner but an odd one that is more like a pie-shaped turn, a less-than-ninety-degree angle. I would usually cut the corner short to save a few precious seconds on the journey home.

Suddenly I heard a voice say, "Don't cut the corner short." It was so natural a sound that I disregarded it. After a pause, I heard it again. The voice wasn't insistent; it just blended in. Finally I heard it a third time, and this time it registered. I felt myself saying, "Okay" internally and slowed the car to take the corner really wide—for the first time ever.

If I hadn't, I would not have seen the lights of the car coming at me until it was too late. It was speeding like a bat out of hell, and there would have been nothing left of either of us but crumpled metal.

The phenomenon of the voice talking to me, not once but three times, seemed as natural as breathing, as the sun shining, as taking one step after another. It was not spooky or strange. It had to have been my angel. More than thirty-five years later I am still grateful for it. And I never again cut that corner short.

—*Casmira, Marlborough, Connecticut*

Angel Touches an Average Life

Your request for small miracles brought to mind an incident that happened—began, actually—a long time ago in Clay Center, Kansas.

It was 1939. I was approached by a man who was selling a correspondence course on how to pass a government job examination. I invested in one of the courses. I studied, passed, and went to work as a messenger for the Veterans Administration regional office in Wichita, Kansas.

I worked my way up from a six-day-a-week, $65-a-month job to a five-day-a-week, $100-a-month position. Very nice for this high school graduate.

From Wichita I advanced to other VA jobs, in Fayetteville, Arkansas, and finally to the position of assistant supply officer in Chillicothe,

Ohio. I worked in a number of positions here and retired in 1975. My wife and I built a life here.

I have always attributed that Clay Center incident in 1939 to an angel in disguise. I never saw him before and never saw him since. I'm eighty now, and as you can see, it's been a good life.

—*Joseph, Chillicothe, Ohio*

Adventure with an Angel

Miracles? Angels? You bet. The angels and I have been pals since I was a child. One incident, however, still amazes me after more than four decades.

I'm a nun, retired now from teaching and in my late seventies (where has the time gone?). In 1952 things were a little different for us sisters, and I needed special permission to visit my family in Milwaukee. I was allowed to and had a great, though brief, visit. I returned to Chicago on the train and was directed to a cab that would return me to our convent.

It was winter and the snow was high, but I quickly realized the cab driver was taking a wrong route. It quickly became frightening when I told him to turn around and he refused. Then he reached back, pulled me halfway into the front seat with him while he told me all the horrible things he was going to do to me. Afterwards he threatened to throw me into the lake.

I was scared and horrified and on the verge of panic. Pray? Of course I prayed. I even tried to open the door and roll out, but the driver kept the lock on and struck me repeatedly.

All of a sudden I noticed out of the corner of my eye a small red car coming up fast alongside the cab. Then I heard a loud—and I do mean loud—man's voice: "Sister, jump. I saw what happened. Run. Run. Run."

The cabbie was distracted and I did exactly that. The two of them fought and the cab driver fled, though not before I had the presence of mind to take down his license number. When the dust settled, my rescuer drove me home.

It was very late and I had no key. The mother superior came to the door, and the man who had come to my aid explained what had happened. She didn't believe him and scolded me right in front of him, accusing me of being "out" with him (I told you things were different then). Anything we said went unheeded.

Only later, when she received a letter of apology from the cab company for the driver's behavior and a check to cover my doctor's bills, did she believe me.

Of course, I know my rescuer was an angel in disguise.

—*Sister Eladia, SSND, Chicago, Illinois*

The Chocolate Angel

I have always loved Psalm 37, especially the part that says, "Delight yourself in the LORD and he will give you the desires of your heart. Commit your way to the LORD; trust in him and he will do this" (Ps. 37:4–5).

I believed it even more after my chocolate angel visited me.

It happened near the end of a long bout of illness. I had developed a very strong, almost irresistible craving for chocolate. But after weeks of being laid up with infectious mononucleosis, I could barely get around the house, let alone to a store. The craving was so powerful that, weak as I was, I scoured the kitchen cabinets for any remains of candy. Alas, not a chocolate chip was to be found.

Not only was I discouraged, I was still craving.

I thought about calling the neighbor who had already done so much for me during the months of my illness. Oh, it was easy to phone and ask her to pick up a gallon of milk or a loaf of bread. But I felt uncomfortable asking her to make a special trip for, of all things, chocolate.

I gave it up and headed back to my couch, when the doorbell rang. It was about one-thirty in the afternoon, and I wasn't expecting anyone. Opening the door, I was surprised to see a young boy, perhaps seven years old. I didn't recognize him as one of the neighborhood youngsters, and he was alone, with no adult in sight. I thought that strange at the moment, but then I noticed he was holding a small box in his hand.

He looked up at me and asked in a sweet way if I would like to buy some chocolate.

Would I ever!

I almost scooped up this little boy, box of chocolate and all, into my arms. I felt a burst of energy, scrounged up one dollar for two bars, and thanked him over and over. He made me happier than he could ever know.

By the time the two bars of candy were just a couple of empty wrappers, I reflected about just how incredible the incident was. A young school-age child, alone with no waiting parent in sight, carrying just what I needed in a dark time—he had to have been an angel.

As I lay on the couch, satisfied and grateful, I thanked God for sending me one of his own to care for me when I needed care.

—*Mary, Downers Grove, Illinois*

The Winter Angel

I've been a shift worker for more than twenty-five years. Anyone who knows shift workers knows they work all sorts of crazy hours in all sorts of weather conditions. I have to go back about twenty years to one night I'll never forget.

It was a cold and threatening winter night, the one thing shift workers like me don't look forward to. The idea of staying up all night working while everyone else is tucked away warm and cozy is not fun. Neither is glancing out the window just before it's time to leave home for work and seeing a snowstorm in progress.

But that was what it was like on this particular night.

I drove an old car in those days, a '61 Comet I had bought from a friend for fifty dollars. I knew that old car like the back of my hand, but the weather was going to be a problem. On the radio, state police were warning against being on the road unless absolutely necessary. Well, it was necessary for me to get to work, so off I went. I figured I'd just take it a little slowly.

The storm was heavy, but I made it from one major highway to another okay. I was about halfway there, praying all the while, when it hit: a whiteout. It was as though someone had taken a white sheet and thrown it over the windshield. I could see nothing and it frightened me. I quickly came to a stop and tried not to panic, but it wasn't easy.

I couldn't see in front or behind me, but I knew I had to move, otherwise someone would surely ram me from the rear. I decided to creep the car slowly along. I remember thinking, *Just keep the car straight.*

I don't know how far I went, but suddenly I felt the car sliding off the road into a ditch, where it stopped. I just sat there at first and got mad. Now what? After about ten minutes of anger and feeling sorry for myself, I decided to grab my lunch box and somehow head for the next exit on foot. I knew there was a gas station there.

I was about to leave the car when there was a soft tap on the window. It was a young man asking if I was okay. He said he had seen me go into the ditch and came over to help. He asked where I was going, and I told him I was heading to work. He explained that his car was just up the road and said that though his tires weren't that good, if he took it easy we'd be all right. I told him that if he'd take me to the gas station, I could get help from there. No, he said, he'd take me all the way to my job.

But what he said next was something I'll never forget. We were just making small talk as we drove along, and he said, "I bet you never believed in angels before, did you?"

I think about that night often, even these many years later. Just the other day I realized something I should have understood immediately: How could he have seen me go into the ditch? Visibility was zero and I'd been there at least ten minutes before he found me.

No, it was truly a miracle. Oh, and I arrived at work that night, right to the back door. Thanks, I guess, to my winter angel.

—*Paul, Joliet, Illinois*

An "Angelo Custode"

Long ago when I was still living in my native Rome, Italy, I came to believe in my "angelo custode," my guardian angel. Or perhaps more correctly, my son's angelo custode.

Claudio, my son, was only two. It was a very hot summer afternoon, and our fifth-floor apartment afforded us only a little breeze through the open window. We were alone in the house. Claudio was sitting on the floor playing with his toys. I was watching him, but it was warm and I was very tired. I fell fast asleep.

I don't know how long I was sleeping. I only know that in the depths of my slumber, I suddenly felt as if a hand were on my left shoulder, shaking me to wake up.

I awakened and immediately my eyes fell on little Claudio standing on a chair in front of the open window. I saw him and I saw the sky beyond him, all frozen in that split second of time. I had the presence of mind not to scream; that could have frightened him and made him tumble from the window. I got up from my chair, dashed the few steps to the window, and grabbed Claudio into my arms.

He was saved, but by whom? Who awoke me just in time?

While I was asleep, Claudio had the time to drag the chair from the kitchen table to the window. I didn't hear a thing. But something—an angel?—shook me awake in time. Through that angel, God touched my life with compassion and love. For he not only saved Claudio, he saved me as well. After all, how could I have forgiven myself if Claudio had fallen to his death?

I'm an old woman now. Claudio is forty-two years old and has two children of his own. But every time I think back to this story, this true story, I tremble with the reality of God's presence demonstrated in such a tangible way.

—*Eugenia, Great Neck, New York*

Lord of the Angels

Sometimes, Lord, we find ourselves in darkness.
The world is closed and frightening. You seem so far away.
   Our troubles seem to block you from our vision.
Yet even then, Lord, you surround us.
   Your light is there to pierce and shatter the darkness.
You gift us, Lord, with those who bear your love, who come as
   your angels, to minister to us.
We are grateful for the gentle touches of your presence.
We are thankful for the ways you allow others to minister to us—
   to be your angels.
Amen.

Nine

In the Presence of Miracles

robably the most famous story in all Christendom is the story of the Prodigal Son. It's such a famous tale that most of us could tell a *Reader's Digest* version. That one goes something like this:

Obnoxious, know-it-all kid thinks life at home is the pits. He wheedles a share of the family fortune and splits for another country, where he celebrates his misspent youth by blowing the loot in short order. Then he gets a lot hungrier, a little smarter, and wants to come home.

Are you with me so far?

The kid is sure his old man will kick him right back out, but he's learned enough to swallow his pride and beg for mercy.

Surprise. The old man is delighted and it's party time at the homestead. Straight-arrow big brother isn't too happy, but who cares? Dad gives him a few pat excuses and he calms down. The end.

Easy, wasn't it? But the reason that the story of the Prodigal Son is so famous is because it really can't be condensed like that. It's a story that touches us on too many levels.

Besides, I can't read the story of the Prodigal Son without thinking of a guy with the unlikely name of Rocky.

That's because Rocky has lived his own version of the Prodigal story. It too is about a boy and his dad. And it too is about God. It's a story of insistence, of rescue, of unqualified presence. And ultimately, it's a story of insight.

But it's also a story about a baseball—and a baseball glove.

Let me tell you about Rocky. Several months before this story takes place, Rocky's only son, who was just fifteen, was killed by a drunken driver in Daytona Beach, Florida, not far from where they lived.

Understandably, the accident devastated Rocky. It hurled him deep into a grief-studded depression. Rocky's father-in-law lived in Cincinnati and was an avid baseball fan. He kept trying to pry Rocky out of his grief by extending an invitation to attend a ball game. And Rocky kept saying no, kept digging his heels deeper into withdrawal.

Why? It was because his son had been a good athlete and a great baseball fan who would have loved to go to such a game. Rocky couldn't bring himself to enjoy it without him. So he kept refusing. The father-in-law's pressure was gentle and persistent. Finally Rocky thought maybe he'd better ask God about his dilemma.

Torn between going and not going, Rocky finally negotiated a deal with the Almighty. At least, that's what he thought he was doing. It was a deal not very much different, I might add, than the deal struck by the Prodigal Son. In both stories, there was a cry to be rescued from the pain and agony of a life situation.

You know the kind of deal I'm talking about, because, if we're honest, we've all done the same thing. Our deals probably go something like, "Okay, God, if I do this, maybe you'll do that. At least, I'll hope you

State. As we had done with each of Michelle's sisters, I visited her and took a few pictures around the campus. The weather wasn't cooperative, so there weren't many opportunities for snapshots.

So we ferried to Victoria, British Columbia, and I used up most of the roll of film there. After leaving Michelle, I continued on across the continent to my sister's home in Louisiana. I noticed I had only one shot left in my camera, so I snapped a picture of a friend and had the film developed at a one-hour photo shop there. Only the photos taken in Victoria had come out and none with Michelle on campus. I was heart-broken, because this had been such a family tradition. Nevertheless, I took some more photos of my sister with fresh film.

Back home in Hawaii the following week, I had the roll of Louisiana pictures developed. Much to my surprise, there were three photos of Michelle on the UW campus. How they came to be on a roll of film bought in Louisiana I don't know. But I'm delighted to preserve that family tradition. To me it's a miracle.

—*Simone, Kailua, Hawaii*

A White Lie Made Good

We were married in 1947 and remained childless for seven years. Oh, how we yearned for a child. When it was apparent that we could not conceive, we applied for adoption at the New York Foundling Home.

We were living in a one-bedroom apartment and knew that would not do. We would have to find an apartment with a separate bedroom for the child. Fortunately, we found one easily enough, but it needed many repairs before we could move in.

My husband was a New York City policeman, and we didn't have a great deal of money. So he did all the work himself in whatever free time a police officer had. But there wasn't much money and there wasn't much time, and we continued to live at the smaller place as the work went on.

When we had applied at the Foundling Home, we used the address of the new apartment, even though we weren't living there yet. We understood how important the separate bedrooms were, and we really wanted a child. So we told a very small white lie. We were sure that by the time the agency got around to us, we'd be long moved in.

Several weeks later I was at work when my husband returned from a midnight-to-eight-a.m. tour of duty. He was dog-tired and went right to bed. But no matter what he did, he couldn't nod off. He just tossed and turned, tossed and turned.

But that's the miracle.

He told me later that he finally sat upright in bed with the very strong feeling to go to our "new" apartment and do some painting. When he got there, he found a letter from the Foundling Home dropped through the mail slot. The letter told us to appear at one p.m. that very day for an important interview. It had been there a week.

Quickly my husband called me, and we made it to the interview just in time. I've often wondered what our lives would be like today if he had gone to sleep and missed the appointment. We would not have had the immense joy and happiness our lovely daughter has given us since. Nor would we be enjoying our two wonderful grandsons.

—*Constance, Queens, New York*

Strange—But Not Phony

Sometimes miracles are so strange that they may seem phony. But I have learned to trust God's promises. That was something that was part of my Lutheran upbringing, and I'm glad of it.

My husband hadn't been feeling well and had been in the hospital for almost a week with chest pains. All the tests ruled out heart trouble. When they couldn't find anything specific, the doctors sent him home for the weekend. There were more tests scheduled for Monday.

Not long after we left for home, the pains returned, stronger than before. He'd received that clear cardiac report, so we ignored them. When they became even more severe, I tried giving him medicine for indigestion. It didn't help and I became very scared.

And that's when our miracle happened.

Unexpectedly, our daughter, a registered nurse, showed up at the door. She'd been relaxing in her apartment one hundred miles away, having a cup of tea, she said, when she felt a powerful urge to be with us. She got into her car and drove to our home.

One look at her father and she knew he was having a heart attack. She took over from there, did all the right treatments, and got him to emergency care. Everything turned out all right.

I know God sent her to us at that moment. Otherwise, he might not have made it.

—*Shirley, Goderich, Ontario, Canada*

Eighty-four Years of Miracles

Ever since I heard about the request for people to share their little miracles, I have been thinking about the many ways in which God has touched my life. I concluded that for me, my entire life has been a "major league," rather than a "small," miracle.

I do not say this lightly. I am eighty-four years old and have had a long life upon which to reflect. I have come to realize that God's presence in my life began long ago.

I don't know too much about my biological family. My mother died when I was about six weeks old. My father, a southern Illinois coal miner, and his brother tried to care for me and my older sister. They couldn't and turned us poor, motherless waifs over to the Children's Home and Aid Society for placement.

I believe it was divine providence that I was adopted into a loving home with three caring adults. In addition to my adoptive parents, there was a niece who had been living with them. They provided me with everything they could possibly afford and more.

I remember the summer before eighth grade, when my adoptive mother became quite ill with typhoid fever and nearly died. The farm economy was very depressed, and she had been earning money with two projects. One was combing her hair and saving the loose strands to sell for the ladies' false hairpieces that were so popular at that time. The other was churning and selling butter to the more affluent residents of our small central Illinois town of Monticello.

Even though the money that the butter brought in was so very important to our family, there was always a small dish of butter in front of my place at the table. At the time, I didn't understand why it was always called "M.'s butter." The others sometimes had margarine, but despite its cost, I always had butter.

In 1929 when the stock market made its famous crash, I discovered that my parents had mortgaged their home to keep me in college. I left immediately and found a job to help out with the finances. I became a home visitor for the Illinois Emergency Relief Organization, a forerunner of our present welfare system.

That's when I first became aware of God's protection. I was to visit a deranged World War I veteran to determine if he would receive one of the new mattresses the agency was distributing. As I interviewed him, he slammed the bolt on the door closed and began to threaten me. Even as I write this now, more than six decades later, I can see his maniacal expression and the reddish glare to his eyes. At the same instant, I heard a voice in my right ear saying, "Stay calm; don't show any fear." The voice was so close and so real, I looked over my shoulder in amazement. But of course there was no one there.

Remain calm I did. I continued the interview as though nothing had happened, walked to the door, and asked him to open it. In a few seconds his wild look softened, and he did as I asked. From then on, whenever someone from our agency visited the man, there was always someone from the local American Legion post along.

But the voice in my ear clearly told me who was watching out for me.

There have been so many times throughout my life when I could look for—and find—God's presence. During the last years of my husband's life, caring for him was time consuming, but we both felt that we never wanted to be placed in a nursing home. I cared for him at home until he died at ninety-five. Whenever emergencies arose, such as when the sump pump failed on Christmas morning, a quick prayer brought assistance from a part-time minister when regular servicemen were taking a day off. It was just another example of how there was always help from unexpected sources, help I've always considered to be miraculous.

—*M., Monticello, Illinois*

A Mother's Peace

When an event so far surpasses coincidence, I believe it can be considered a small miracle. Such is the following story. My friend Zita had a brother, the last born to the family, who was profoundly retarded. Their mother, Nora, a woman of great faith, did not rail against God for this "injustice" but felt that although her son's condition was a great tragedy, it had a reason in God's grand plan.

The son was cared for lovingly at home until he became a young adult, when he had to be institutionalized. Still, Nora continued to care lovingly. She was at the home every day and even volunteered in the sewing room until she was well past seventy and diagnosed with a malignant brain tumor. Nora had lived her life for her son, caring for him as best as she could, always hoping that she would live beyond him, lest he be abandoned or not cared for properly. Even as she lay dying, her foremost thought was her fear of leaving her son alone.

My friend nursed her mother as the end neared. On the morning of the day Nora would die, her son was found dead in his bed at the home. He had not been ill, and death was totally unexpected. His mother, near death herself and unable to speak, was told of his death. Zita said a look of complete peace spread across her mother's face and she raised her arm in an arc as if to say, "It is consummated." She died within the hour.

—*Patricia, Waterford, Connecticut*

A Family Miracle

When my father was an eleven-year-old boy, he fell off a moving train, severing his left leg below the knee. He used a crutch until he was grown—and still managed to become a pretty accomplished one-legged baseball player. Later he walked with an artificial leg.

During the Great Depression, Daddy was in his mid-fifties and working on WPA (Works Progress Administration) projects, building new roads. His artificial leg was just about worn out, and there was no money to pay for a new one.

One day, a coworker told Daddy about a miraculous find—a brand-new artificial leg that a friend of his had discovered along the very highway they were building. My father really didn't think there was much use in checking it out. After all, the leg would have had to have been made for a man about his height, with the same sort of amputation. But he asked anyway.

Miraculously, the leg fit perfectly. It even had a movable ankle, the first he'd ever had. It was the best artificial leg he ever wore. The only adjustment was that Daddy wore a size eight shoe; the leg's foot was a seven and a half. No problem; just a bit of newspaper in the toe of his shoe.

—*Anne, Covington, Kentucky*

Finding Faith in Unlikely Places

In 1980 the cold war was still very much with us. East Germany was even more dreary than it is now. Tourists—especially American ones—were rare. But it was Christmas day, and our family was visiting my husband's mother for the holidays.

We had attended Lutheran services on Christmas Eve, but in the morning, my husband's uncle and I went to a local Catholic church for what I thought would be the nine a.m. mass. However, when we got there, all the doors were locked. So we sat in his car praying, me in English and Hans in German.

I had brought Hans a gift, a decal for his car of the ancient Christian symbol of a fish. He had gratefully put it on his bumper. There had been an elaborate booklet that went with the decal and explained the history of the symbol. But I had forgotten the booklet when we packed and had left it home in Delaware.

As we prayed in the car that Christmas morning, there was a tap on the driver's-side window. Hans rolled down the window, and a blond

❧

God Who Welcomes

Life's road is often a bumpy one, Lord, paved
    with broken stones and rough spots.
There are corners of darkness when you seem absent, Lord.
Yet you are a surprising God, a God who reveals himself
    in story, adventure, and event.
You are there when we hurt; you are present in the people we
meet;
    you are always ready to welcome us into your love.
Lord, it is that welcome that we seek and crave. Help us
    to have the faith and trust always to accept your welcoming
    word.
Amen.

Ten

※

The Miracle of Being
Lost and Found Again

This is a story about small things.

We like to think of ourselves as "big-picture people," but when you come right down to it, it's the small things in life that build us up—or drag us down.

That's understandable. Big things are usually those that we can do the least about. War and peace. Taxes. Disasters. Even health. That's why it's easier to turn those big things, those big problems, over to God. They have a momentum all their own.

Smaller things—real, in-your-face things—well, they're tougher. These are things we feel we ought to be able to control, ought to be able to take care of. They're what our parents always told us we'd have to handle when we grew up. Remember? But now that we're grown, we're far less likely to turn over these smaller, more intimate things to God.

Our internal discussions usually go something like this: *Okay, God. You worry about world peace and refugees and hurricanes and all that stuff. Let me worry about me. Okay? We got a deal on that, God?* And then we hope God sees it our way.

Otherwise, we can't be sure it'll turn out the way we want it to. When we give away control of small things, we chance becoming vulnerable. So here's a story about something small—a bit of broken wooden spoon, to be precise. And about being vulnerable. The story-teller is Dorothy, a retired religious sister living in Charleston, West Virginia. She's ninety-eight years old.

"It happened years and years ago at a retreat house in Chicago. I was just a young sister, busy as a bee, trying to keep up with the hundreds of people who came morning, noon, and night for prayer, meetings, and the like. I was kept busy—and I don't mean maybe.

"My assignment was to make dessert for all those people—sometimes two and three groups meeting at the same time in different rooms of the house. I was not a gifted cook, but I was blessed with good feet and could stand for most of the day. So my job became the preparation of dessert, a task that usually meant lots of mixing, stirring, and pouring. Not to mention hours of standing.

"Layer cake was our specialty. It was the easiest way to serve the greatest number of people. But it was nearly impossible to mix enough for so many groups—unless I did it all at the same time. Other duties—and prayers, of course—had to fit in, too. So I often worked late at night when it was quieter.

"With a wooden spoon—and with my arms up to the elbow—I mixed the gooey batter as quickly as possible. There was no time for mistakes; no time to do it over. Layers had to be poured into shallow pans, baked, then iced, one after another.

"Late one night, when I was especially pinched for time, I suddenly noticed that the wooden spoon I was using had broken. A big chunk was gone. I realized it was lost somewhere in the batter and was aghast at the potential implications. I tried to fish around with my hands in the big, batter-filled dishpan, but it was useless. I had no more time to waste; there were too many more cakes to bake.

"But later that night, lying in bed, I continued to worry about the lost piece of wooden spoon. Where was it? Someone could choke on the cake. Lord have mercy. Fearfully I watched all the next day as meal after meal, including cake, was served to all those people. Where, I wondered, was the wood?"

But in the end, all Dorothy could do was pray—and apprehensively, at that.

Dorothy felt very vulnerable throughout her weekend ordeal, waiting for the bit of spoon to turn up. Being vulnerable is very uncomfortable. That's because it's our nature to resist vulnerability, to reject it and to keep things—and people—at a distance. We want to keep the "personal space" around us full of things we can control; we really don't like surprises that threaten it. The richer and more powerful we are, the bigger and more inviolate our space. Watch celebrities. They don't wait in line or in crowds. They have escorts to clear and extend their space. Likewise, the poorer and less powerful we are, the less space we command. And the more vulnerable we are.

Most of us are somewhere in the middle, neither very rich nor very poor. But still we seek to reduce our vulnerability. Yet the call to be a Christian is to struggle with control, to forfeit it to God, to become vulnerable, less powerful. Is it any wonder that Christianity has been called a faith of counterculture? It is any wonder that whatever we give up we want to snatch back to make sure things go our way? Dorothy certainly thought so that dark night, throwing herself into the cake batter in search of what had been lost. But she also remembered about prayer and about giving God room to work.

So what happened to that small piece of spoon lost in the batter?

Sunday evening, after all the visitors had gone home, the resident staff sat down to dinner. They served themselves the last few leftover pieces of cake. That small piece of wood, that piece of the spoon that had troubled the young woman so much throughout the weekend, turned up. It was in the last piece of cake, served by the woman who had made the batter—served to herself.

She told me she would never forget that moment. She said, "I'm ninety eight years old now, and that was a long, long time ago. But I still remember. I said, 'Thank you, God.' And then I got goose bumps."

That was what—seventy or eighty years ago? And she still remembers the goose bumps.

Paying attention to small miracles will always promise you goose bumps. It happens whenever we become vulnerable enough to let God come close.

We most often feel vulnerable when we lose things—or lose our way, even if only figuratively. But that sense of loss—even when it seems debilitating—is also an opportunity to allow God to "find" us. That's a grand part of Christian tradition. Jesus told a powerful parable of seeking the things that were lost and celebrating their rediscovery.

> "Suppose one of you has a hundred sheep and loses one of them. Does he not leave the ninety-nine in the open country and

go after the lost sheep until he finds it? And when he finds it, he joyfully puts it on his shoulders and goes home. Then he calls his friends and neighbors together and says, 'Rejoice with me; I have found my lost sheep.'" (LUKE 15:4–6)

Many times we become lost. Sometimes it's a physical ache, sometimes an emotional one. But in all these instances, we seek the miracle of being found again.

A Search-and-Rescue Rescue

I have never told anyone what happened to me in November 1971. Not even my wife. But I've never forgotten a bit of it, not a single detail.

I was a volunteer search-and-rescue pilot with the Civil Air Patrol flying out of Duluth, Minnesota. It was on October 29 that we were called out on a mission to locate a missing float plane with two people and their dog on board. It had disappeared after leaving a lake on the border between Minnesota and Canada, heading for Devil Track Lake in Grand Marais, Minnesota.

The weather was not cooperating; conditions were generally poor, with snow and cold. The search went on for days, with no success. I was dispatched with a crew of two to search along the Canadian border. Because I really wanted to find the plane, we lingered in the search area longer than we should have. Fuel was low, but it would have been enough for us to safely get back, except that the weather turned sour. On the way back to Devil Track Lake, we ran into heavy snow, with a very low ceiling and poor visibility.

Since I was not instrument rated for flying in such conditions, I was hesitant to climb above the clouds. There I would at least be able to remain level, but I could easily become lost when out of sight of the ground. The weather quickly worsened. I had no choice other than soaring higher. The landmarks were lost in the swirling storm below. I was already low on fuel and now had virtually no chance to make any airport, even with clear skies. Our chances of survival quickly became slim.

Just as I was getting frantic and almost ready to give up hope, I recalled my childhood religious instructions about praying in times of danger. I had repeated no more than six or seven words of a familiar verse when the plane soared into a small clear area and I could see the ground through a hole in the clouds. I brought the craft lower.

I felt relieved, of course, but it was clear our problems were still not over. This was very rough and isolated country. I had lost sight of my landmarks when I gained altitude. There were few roads in the area, and I had no idea how to find the landing strip. Then I realized the craft had come down over a clearing I had checked out the day before. I recognized it because of the fresh logging and was able to spot the trail leading back to the airport.

The snow was still falling and the visibility was still poor. But the help was enough; we landed safely at the airport with empty fuel tanks. I know in my heart it was a miracle—it was my miracle.

—*Dave, West Des Moines, Iowa*

Seeing Clearly

On their way to Disney World for a vacation, my brother and his family faced the horror of disaster as a huge semi-truck roared up behind them and ran them right off the highway near the small central-Kentucky town of Glasgow. No one was killed in the shattering crash, thank God, but they were all hurt, his wife and two daughters worse than the others.

Their son Eric, who was only six, has had poor eyesight from birth. His glasses, specially made in New York, were lost in the accident, knocked from his head by the force of the crash. They didn't turn up in the crumpled wreckage of the car. Badly bruised but otherwise okay, Eric and his dad had to wait in a local hotel while the rest of the family recovered in a hospital. Eric, with no glasses, was reduced to sitting for hours on end, staring blankly into empty space. Usually an energetic child, he couldn't see to play. He couldn't even watch cartoons on the hotel TV.

As soon as we got the call about the accident, my husband and I piled into our car and headed for Glasgow. It took us hours to drive the hundreds of miles to be with them, but in the meantime the townspeople there were wonderful. The accident and Eric's unhappy situation had made the local paper, and many people had scoured the crash site, looking for the glasses. But they had no success.

Right after we arrived in town and checked on our family, my husband insisted on making another search. Because we didn't know exactly where the crash had taken place, we stopped at a Glasgow gas station for directions. Sitting out front were several men in rocking chairs. We explained that we wanted to go and find Eric's missing glasses. "You won't find 'em," one of the men said. The rest nodded in agreement. "Lots of us have searched. No luck."

Finally we convinced one of them that we were serious. He escorted us to the scene in his pickup truck, and we began digging in the thick, red Kentucky clay. Three minutes later out popped Eric's glasses. And in good shape.

Eric put them on and whooped with joy. The man from town couldn't believe what had happened. But my husband, who had prayed quietly before setting out, turned to him and said, "Nobody asked the right person for help." Off we drove with Eric and his red-clay glasses, to comfort the rest of the family.

—*Margaret, DeKalb, Illinois*

Child's Journey Has a Silver Lining

It was the Depression, and my father was out of work. Our family was forced to take welfare. Even so, there was little money, barely enough to subsist on.

I was only nine years old. There was going to be a puppet show at school. My oldest sister wanted very much to see it. There wasn't much in the way of entertainment available then, and the puppet show would have been great fun. However, it would have cost each of us a dime to get in. Not much now, but for a child back then, ten cents was a lot. And twenty cents for the two of us was a fortune.

We asked Mother if we could go, but she said we needed the money for food. That was much more important than a puppet show, she said.

My sister and I both understood—grudgingly, since we knew we would have enjoyed the show.

Because our family was on welfare, it was my job to get up early each morning and walk the five blocks from our home to what was called a "milk station" to get free milk. My five-block walk took me past a row of stores. One was a grocery store that sold butter out of small barrels. Each morning, the clerks would put the empty barrels along the curb, to be picked up with the rest of the trash.

That morning it was still nearly dark. As I walked past the grocery, I saw an empty butter barrel at the curb, waiting for the garbagemen. I also spotted something glowing, like a sparkle, inside the barrel. Of course, with my nine-year-old curiosity, I was drawn to investigate.

Peering inside, I saw two dimes stuck upright in the rancid, buttery scum at the bottom of the barrel. Quickly I snatched up the greasy coins and jammed them into my pocket. After getting the milk for the family, I hurried home. I told Mother what had happened. I could see the tears in her eyes, and I knew she understood.

We got to go to the puppet show after all. Deep in my heart, I know that God was smiling on my sister and me when I found those coins. And as you can see, I haven't forgotten that small miracle, even after all these years.

—*Frank, Lindenhurst, New York*

The Cat Who Came In from the Cold

One cold and blustery afternoon when our oldest son, Ron, was ten, he came in from school and left the front door open a split second too long. His black-and-white pal Scribbles the cat slithered through the narrow gap and darted out into the snowy Illinois winter.

It was cold but Ron knew he had to find his cat. He quickly shed his school outfit, bundled up in warmer clothes, and bolted outside to search. Nearly an hour later he returned, chilled to the bone and catless. Scribbles was nowhere to be found. We feared for her life.

That evening, after dinner, Ron insisted on going back out into the cold. He returned about an hour later, frozen again, but this time he had his friend Scribbles under his arm.

Ron told me he looked under bushes and in dark corners, with no success. Then he started to pray, even though he was almost certain that even God couldn't help. No sooner did he finish praying, however, than he heard Scribbles meowing. Looking down, he saw the cat running right beside him.

That evening, after everyone was warmed up—including Scribbles—we sat down to talk about how God answers prayers. We were certainly glad Ron's pet was found—and that prayers helped. Still, we wanted Ron to understand that God doesn't always answer that quickly, and doesn't always answer the way we want. Ron said he understood. I was glad, because I didn't want him to be disappointed the next time something like that happened.

Well, it did. Two or three winters later we had a rerun: same situation, same cat, same blustery weather. Scribbles again slipped out and Ron again went looking for him. He returned much later, frozen again and with Scribbles in his arms. I was so happy to see them both, I didn't say a word. Ron just looked at me, smiled, and said, "It worked again."

—*Joy, Naperville, Illinois*

Locked Out!

I grew up in a South Dakota farming community where pheasant hunting was a yearly sport. I still enjoy going back each October to hunt with my younger brothers and other kin. Though it was hard to flush out many birds on this particular fall day because the area is crop-rest acreage, we covered lots of ground and managed to get our limit. My nephew Bob drove us back to town to clean and freeze the birds.

When I went to start my car, I discovered that my entire key ring was missing, having fallen through a hole in my jacket pocket. The keys must have slipped to the ground while we were tramping over the farmland.

If it had been only the car key, it might not have been quite so bad. But on the same ring were keys to both of our family cars, a key to the town fire department, where I am a member, house keys, and keys to a bank safety deposit box and home lockbox. It wasn't like losing the keys to the kingdom, but it would be a terrible blow just the same. Costly to replace, too.

The land we had hunted was off an infrequently traveled country road with lots of grass and weeds along it. The fields too were overgrown. We went back to look but gave up after a while, reconciled that the keys were lost for good.

The sleepless night passed, and I knew I had to try once more. Bob and I retraced our steps yet again. We had walked along the road and in the weeds again and again. Nothing. There was no way I was going to find those keys. Disappointed and upset, we drove back to town.

Bob dropped me off but explained later that he felt an urge to go back out for just one more look. This time, miraculously, he quickly spotted the keys openly lying in the weeds—the same weeds where we had looked so many times before. Don't tell me that God isn't with us all the time. He performed the "miracle of the keys" for me.

—Gerald, Manteno, Illinois

A Memory and a Marker

My sister Normandie died in 1939 when she was two. Our family buried her in a cemetery near the town where we lived. As the years passed, I married and moved away. About ten years later we returned to the area and decided to visit little Normandie's grave. I knew there was a headstone, but after searching and searching, we couldn't find it. Finally we gave up.

A few years passed, and in 1953 my husband and I had a daughter. We named her Normandie. It seemed like a special thing to do. In her teens she too wanted to find her namesake's gravesite and, though she searched many times, could not. In 1974 she was married. Without realizing it, she chose October 12, Normandie's birthday, for her wedding.

Sadly, the marriage lasted less than a year. On the day that would have been her first anniversary, she was instead in the midst of the divorce and feeling very down. It was such a beautiful autumn Sunday that I suggested a drive to see if we could find her namesake's grave and headstone. I thought it would help lift her sagging spirits. But again we had no luck.

Disappointed, I turned to Normandie, who was searching through old markers about forty feet away, and said, "Come on, honey, we're never going to find it." But as I spoke the words, a slight breeze blew between us and stirred the leaves off a small gravestone. Normandie looked down and cried out, "Mom! Here it is."

And it was. What was lost had been found. At a very needful time.

—*Lorraine, Lake Tomahawk, Wisconsin*

A Gem of a Christmas

My husband, Tom, surprised me with an engagement ring on Christmas in 1938. It was very precious to me. Not for the diamond but for the memories and the meaning.

In 1980 I was a church secretary in West Chicago, Illinois. Typing away one day, I noticed, to my horror, the diamond gone from the setting of my ring. I didn't even know when—or where—I'd lost it, so I searched the chair, the desk, the floor, my car, at home—all with no success. After several weeks I became reconciled to never finding the stone.

I retired later that year. Just before Christmas of the following year, I was asked if I could help out by pressing the large altar cloth the church used for holiday-season services. "Sure," I said, intending to bring it home to iron. On second thought, however, I took the cloth instead into the church's laundry room. I could do the job there and save myself an extra trip, I reasoned.

As I carefully ironed the wrinkles out of that big altar cloth, in preparation for the miracle of Christmas, my eyes fell on an old secretarial chair. It was the one I had used for many years. It had been retired along with me and sat, forlorn, in a deserted corner of the laundry room.

I still can't explain the sudden little voice that seemed to say, "Look in that chair again for your diamond." I ran my fingers along the edge of the seat, deep into the creases, and caught, to my amazement, the glint of a gemstone.

When I joyously told the pastor later what had happened, he said they had tried to get rid of that old chair many times since I left. But each time, it always ended up being rescued from the trash heap. Now I know why. What a wonderful Christmas miracle.

—*Alice, West Chicago, Illinois*

Miracle in the Mind's Eye

It happened in Lithuania in 1933. I returned from high school to my parents' farm for summer vacation. My mother was busy in the kitchen, and I had to go to work in the field. As I left, I slipped my father's pocketknife into my pocket. I just wanted to borrow it for a while.

But after completing my chores and coming home, I discovered that the knife was missing. It was terrible; I had lost my father's favorite knife. I knew losing it would create a long squabble between us. Mother would also be blamed, since it had been on her table when I took it.

What could I do? I prayed, though I didn't know whether it would do any good.

Suddenly a picture formed in my mind, of about a square meter of land in the field where I had been working. The knife was there; I knew it. I recognized the image in my mind. I leaped out the open window and sprinted the three hundred meters to the spot. The knife was there, exactly as I had pictured it. I was touched suddenly by the inner feeling that I was not alone in the field. My desperate prayers had been answered.

—*V. M., Etobicoke, Ontario, Canada*

Lord of the Lost

We wander, we lose our way.
We stumble in darkness; we struggle. Lord of the lost, guide us.
Lord, too often we lose sight—
    of our path . . .
    of our faith . . .
    of the things of this life . . .
We hurt, we fear, we panic.
But in you, Lord, we can find ourselves.
Hard it is to trust that a God who loves us truly will help us.
We don't like to be that dependent, that vulnerable, that
    trusting.
    But we try.
When we are lost, Lord, gently remind us that you—
    and only you—are the Lord of the lost.
Amen.

Eleven

❧

Do You Have a Miracle to Tell?

Shortly before this book was completed, I received a printed announcement in the mail. It was an obituary. At first I couldn't figure out why I had received it; I didn't seem to know the woman who had died. But then I recalled the letter she had written months earlier in response to my nationwide call for small miracles.

Hers was a remarkable story of following the will of God, a story that took her from agnostic to believer to medical missionary serving God and healing his people. I had already intended to include the miracles of her life in this book. But my first thought was: Wow. Pretty impressive that someone in her circle of friends would remember that she had responded to the invitation to tell her miracles, and would let me know about her death.

My second thought, however, was: Does this mean that the miracles of her life are over?

The answer came immediately: Of course not.

That's the final truth of miracles—once we are part of miracles, once we have recognized them, they cannot be separated from us. Once we have shared them with others, they are eternal.

Paula Therese Starke was diagnosed with cancer a few months after writing her life's miracles for others to read.

This is her story.

A Life Full of Miracles

Small miracles? How about a complex one?

Many years ago I dreamed of becoming a physician. But women in medicine were almost unknown way back before World War II. So there I was, a senior in college and a math major. The dream happened for me because a boy I was dating—a medical student—had invited me to a medical seminar with him.

Instantaneously I knew what I wanted to do with my life: I wanted to go to medical school. However, I had taken no premed courses. Oh, I'd had some science, but not enough. My teachers, however, were supportive, so I applied to four medical schools. Three were quick with their replies: no, no, and no.

Even an agnostic, which is what I was, can pray. My prayer went like this: "Dear God, if you exist, please get me into medical school and let me become a doctor, and I promise I'll never ask to be married."

The fourth college replied: yes. That was a miracle in itself, because very few students without premed training were admitted. And at that time, women made up only one percent of the class.

I loved every minute of medical school. I also fell in love with a classmate. We planned to be married after our training. He was offered an internship in one hospital, and I in another. During my internship, I received a letter from him. It was a strange letter in which he told me he loved me but didn't think we should marry. He would instead wed a girl from Boston.

The news hit me very hard. I suffered from depression for about a year, though I managed to continue my medical school studies. It hurt me so much that I never remembered the bargain I had made with God. After all, I was still an agnostic.

At last, though, my dream came true: I was a physician. A few years later I had a patient who was a priest from Brooklyn. He was quite ill and even brought a nursing nun to help him. During their stay in the city for his treatment, I invited the nun to dinner, because I was curious about faith. I remember that during the meal, I bombarded her with question after question. Some of these she answered well, but she seemed a bit uncertain of others.

It was obvious that she discussed me with her patient, because soon afterward three books on faith arrived in the mail. The books addressed the sorts of questions an agnostic would ask. They talked about discovering God by using reason and reality, not just fancy religious words. I read them.

I became a believer.

Three years later I took vows as a Roman Catholic nun in the Maryknoll order. Only then did I remember my promise to remain unwed, made to a God I wasn't even certain existed. For many years I had the unique privilege of working in academic medicine, a major thrust of Maryknoll. When I turned seventy, it was time to leave that field. But I was again involved in a miracle: I was blessed to be able to work in a clinic for indigent patients in Houston.

So here I am, more than six years later, still going strong, still struggling with communicating in Spanish, still doing God's work and healing people. It's a wonderful place for me to be. God knows how long he wants me to continue.

—*Paula, Houston, Texas*

This is how her community of friends and fellow missionaries remembered her after her death in July 1995: "Paula Therese was a woman of strong faith. She was a woman of her church, which was the framework for her life. Her energy, time, and medical skills were given to the church and God's people. This is what Paula felt gave meaning to her life."

I never knew—never really knew—Paula Therese Starke. But I knew her story. And because she told that story, I knew a part of her. No, her miracles are not forgotten. They are not overshadowed by death. That is the power of God at work.

❧

So far, nearly two thousand people have responded to this invitation. If you have a story to tell, a touch of God, an awakening, a miracle, please share it. It is how God becomes present.

Wanted: Small Miracles

Do you know a small miracle? I believe most people do, if they really think about it. Not necessarily a major-league miracle like water turning into wine, or the Red Sea parting. Just the everyday sort that lets us know God is alive and well—a moment when God touches our lives.

I'm inviting people from all over to tell their miracles. It might be something that seems unimportant—except to you—perhaps a healing, an insight, an event, or even an opportunity. Please share them with me.

Tom Sheridan
Small Miracles
Box 3003–120
Naperville, IL 60566

❧

I will praise you, O LORD, with all my heart;
I will tell of all your wonders.

—Ps. 9:1